# Rendezvous in Paris

# Rendezvous in Paris

BARRY BLACKSTONE

RESOURCE *Publications* · Eugene, Oregon

RENDEZVOUS IN PARIS

Copyright © 2010 Barry Blackstone. All rights reserved. Except for brief quotations in critical publications or reviews, no part of this book may be reproduced in any manner without prior written permission from the publisher. Write: Permissions, Wipf and Stock Publishers, 199 W. 8th Ave., Suite 3, Eugene, OR 97401.

Resource Publications
An Imprint of Wipf and Stock Publishers
199 W. 8th Ave., Suite 3
Eugene, OR 97401

ISBN 13: 978-1-60899-346-8

Manufactured in the U.S.A.

*I dedicate this series of practical observations and personal opinions to my dearest daughter, Marnie Lee, and to the extraordinary experience and spiritual insight we shared together in our "Rendezvous in Paris!"*

## Contents

Prelude • *xi*

1. Getting on the Bus • 1
2. A Deaf Ride • 3
3. Come Apart • 5
4. I'll Meet You in Paris • 8
5. A Letter to Co • 11
6. From Portland to Philly • 13
7. What is Man? • 15
8. All Routes Lead to Paris • 17
9. Philadelphia • 19
10. The View from the Window • 21
11. Marvelous Machines • 23
12. To Sit and Think • 25
13. Delayed Flight • 27
14. Stranger in Service • 29
15. Trusting the Pilot • 31
16. One Ocean, One God • 33
17. 13 Days in October • 35
18. Joshua's Day • 37

| | | |
|---|---|---|
| 19 | Joy Comes in the Morning • | 39 |
| 20 | The Shadow of Your Smile • | 41 |
| 21 | African Feet • | 43 |
| 22 | A Piece of Our Heart • | 45 |
| 23 | De Gaulle Airport to De Mars Tour Eiffel • | 47 |
| 24 | Ice Cream at the Eiffel Tower • | 49 |
| 25 | Downtown Park • | 51 |
| 26 | The Eiffel Tower • | 53 |
| 27 | Unimpressed with Paris • | 55 |
| 28 | Detour • | 57 |
| 29 | Pooped Out in Paris • | 59 |
| 30 | Old Cathedrals • | 61 |
| 31 | Speaking One to Another • | 63 |
| 32 | Open Window • | 65 |
| 33 | Heading Home • | 68 |
| 34 | 24 Hours • | 70 |
| 35 | "The Kid" • | 72 |
| 36 | Winging on West • | 74 |
| 37 | Blessed Downcastings • | 76 |
| 38 | Borrow Tomorrow? • | 78 |
| 39 | Sufficient • | 80 |
| 40 | Eloquent Etiquette • | 82 |
| 41 | The Testimony of a Tourist • | 84 |
| 42 | Watering Weeds • | 86 |
| 43 | Leaving Leaves • | 88 |

| | | |
|---|---|---|
| 44 | Redeeming the Time | • 91 |
| 45 | Checklist for Takeoff | • 94 |
| 46 | African Jewel | • 96 |
| 47 | Ten Days of Miracles | • 99 |
| 48 | A Fly on the Flight | • 101 |
| 49 | Forty Hours | • 103 |
| 50 | His Purpose | • 106 |
| | Postlude | • 109 |

## Prelude

I must say with the Psalmist, "... my tongue is the pen of a ready writer" (Psalms 45:1). If my tongue were a pen, oh, what truth I could proclaim, but it is not my tongue but my heart that is writing now!

I am on a Concord Trail ways' bus heading south for Boston. My mind is filled with hundreds of details, and my soul is full with a thousand emotions as I journey. I can't help but write down my observations, and hopefully my inspirations. Perhaps that is why I am going to Paris to meet my daughter, Marnie. I tell myself that I am going to meet her so she won't have to travel home alone. I know she could. Wasn't it four years ago that, at the age of seventeen, she traveled alone from Nigeria in Africa, through Amsterdam, to her home in Maine? Now she is twenty-one and a senior in college, so why am I going? I believe because the Good Lord has directed my feet and prepared my heart for a forty-hour, round-trip odyssey to Paris, France, and back.

Marnie got sick on this her second summer in Africa. In 1997 she had spent fifty-nine days in Nigeria with a missionary couple from our church. This summer's mission trip to West Africa covered forty-four days, but the difference is that on this adventure, Marnie contracted malaria and picked up a parasite. She became violently ill ten days ago and had to be hospitalized. According to the doctor and nurse that have been caring for her, she is better but very weak. My wife thought it would be nice if a traveling companion could be arranged for the trip home. Within the week, the Lord worked out the tickets, the financing, and my expired passport, so now I am on my way to Logan Airport to catch a plane to Philadelphia, then on to Paris before this day is through.

In our last phone call from Togo, Marnie said she could do it alone. The lady she was staying with thought Marnie was well enough to travel, yet here I am with my tickets in hand, heading to Europe to meet my daughter at the Charles De Gaulle Aero port. Within I hear the "still, small voice" of God saying, "I will show you why you are going. I need you alone; trust my leading with an open heart. There are lessons and devotions and sermons I need to give you, and you will only understand and receive them if you follow me to Paris!" So, I travel on with only God as companion.

I have never felt such peace about anything, even though my logical mind says it is a waste of time and money. This is so unlike me, and probably if not motivated by the "apple of my eye," I would not be taking this trip. So sit back and relax, for contained in this devotional are the many challenges the Lord Jesus Christ showed me through my "Rendezvous in Paris." I will probably never again write a book quite like this one. All the devotions you will read were either written or inspired in a span of only forty hours in the summer of 2001.

Barry Blackstone
July 25, 2001

1

## Getting on the Bus

I HAVE JUST TAKEN my seat on a bus heading for Logan Airport in Boston. Believe it or not, despite being fifty years old, this will be my very first commercial bus ride. I am taking the bus because it is the best way to get to my airline connections on time. I will not be returning by bus, so for me to take my car to Logan would be a waste. I will, the Lord willing, be returning with my daughter, Marnie, who left Togo, West Africa, just a few short hours ago. She had gotten sick on a short-term missions trip to that hot and disease-filled land, and I am heading out now to rendezvous with her in Paris. Hopefully I will fly back home tomorrow with her. But this forty-hour adventure began with my dear wife, Coleen, putting me on a bus in Bangor, Maine.

It has been twenty-nine years since I last flew overseas, so to say that I am completely comfortable with this trip would be wrong. I am way out of my comfort zone, to say the least, but the Lord has directed very clearly that I should go to Paris—so, to Paris I will go. My emotions at this moment are similar to those expressed by one of John Bunyan's characters in "Pilgrim's Progress." Remember, Mr. Fearing was a believer who feared day and night that he would never arrive safely at his destination. For my trip to Paris, I have brought along an old friend to read: a 1973 copy of Vance

Havner's classic devotional, "Song at Twilight." In that book, he writes this about Mr. Fearing:

> A timid soul, he never dared claim with certainty many joys he might have known. As MacClaren put it, "He managed to distill bitter vinegar of self-accusation out of grand words in the Bible that were meant to afford the wine of gladness and of consolation." He trembled when he should have triumphed, sighed when he should have sung. But he had the root of the matter in him and Bunyan tells us that when Mr. Fearing finally reached the river it was at its lowest and he got across "not much above wet-shod."

This is my determination on this unexpected trip to Paris and back, no matter what: to not be a Mr. Fearing! I am going to claim in this "first mile of the way" a wonderful Biblical instruction:

> Trust in the Lord with all thine heart; and lean not unto thine own understanding. In all they ways acknowledge Him, and He shall direct thy path. (Proverbs 3:5–6)

In the "last mile of the way," may I be singing, not sighing!

So as Fred, the Concord Trail way's driver, drives me down the Maine interstate, I am going to sit back, relax, and leave the decisions and directions to my heavenly Father. I have gotten on the bus—that was my responsibility. Now I am going to place my faith in His all-knowing hands and trust that He will get me to my rendezvous on time. Unlike Mr. Fearing, I am going to enjoy the journey to the destination!

## 2

## A Deaf Ride

WHEN I BOARDED THE Concord Trail ways bus in Bangor, Maine, I was asked if I wanted any earphones so I could listen to music or watch the onboard movie—"Rugrats in Paris." It was a fitting flick, seeing as I was heading to Paris myself. I refused the earphones, however, for I prefer to listen to my Traveling Companion rather than the sounds of the world. It's not because I am pious or too good to watch or listen; I am still trying to figure out why my heavenly Father is sending me to Paris for a rendezvous with my daughter.

Part of the joy of being a Christian, I believe, is being able to listen to God. Hearing His "still, small voice," whether through His Word or His Spirit, is a blessing beyond description. I am only a few hours into my odyssey, and I have heard a lot from Him already. His is a soothing, satisfying voice. He has already calmed my fears and doubts about this adventure. He has told me to sit back, enjoy the ride, and leave the driving and flying to Him, and that's exactly what I'm doing!

This quiet drive to Boston has reminded me just how this world in which I'm living has become accustomed to hearing aids of all sorts. My traveling companions believe they can't hear anything without earphones, headsets, and amplifiers. It reminds me of what Jesus said, ". . . hearing, they hear not, neither do they understand" (Matthew 13:13). Our problem isn't that we are deaf, but that we don't want to take the time to listen to God; "Rugrats in Paris" is much more entertaining! So instead of listening for God, we shut Him out with our movies and our music. God is talking, but are we listening?

I have come to a place in my life where I abhor all new communication devices: cell phones (I am determined to be the last person on this planet without a cell phone), CD players, digital television, etc, etc! They are only more gadgets to keep me from listening to God. "And he said unto them, 'He that hath ears to hear, let him hear'" (Mark 4:9). It isn't that we don't want to hear; it is that we want to hear what we want to hear. When was the last time we were admonished by, "He that hath an ear, let him hear what the Spirit saith . . . ?" (Revelation 2:7). I am determined to take the next 40 hours (flying to Paris and back) and spend the bulk of it listening to the Spirit and the Scriptures. I like the way Vance Havner put it:

> Something has gone wrong with our hearing—both physically and spiritually. We are not going to correct it by clever devices. We must get at the cause. We need to do something about how we hear as well as what we hear. There is a famine of the hearing of the Word . . . because our ears are not tuned and trained to hear it. God grant us more Samuels who can say, "Speak, Lord, for thy servant heareth." (1 Samuel 3:9)

I want to be a Samuel on this trip to Paris!

## 3

## Come Apart

I AM ON A God-ordained mission!

By my very nature, I am the adventurous type, and when you have a daughter who is adventurous as well, sometimes you get caught up in her adventures. Such is the case as I write these thoughts from a Concord Trail ways bus heading from Bangor, Maine to Boston, Massachusetts. My daughter and I are scheduled to meet in fourteen hours at Terminal #1 in the Charles de Gaulle Aero port in Paris, France. In the meantime, I am writing through the bumps of a bus, not an ideal writing platform. Still, I am led to write about this adventure and to highlight and underline the lessons the Lord shares with me as I travel. As I write Marnie is on a plane out of Africa: Lome, West Africa to be exact. Marnie has been forty-four days in that hostile land doing Child Evangelism Fellowship work with three ladies of God named Judy, Sharon, and Becky. I will forever be thankful to them and many other unnamed angels who have helped my daughter through a terrible experience with malaria and a parasite. I would have meet Marnie in Lome if I could, but there were no more seats on the flight, so Paris is the closest place we can rendezvous.

This being my first time on a commercial bus, I didn't know what to expect. My first observation is that people pretty much keep to themselves on the bus. I am riding with about twenty other people, and no one has yet spoken. The seat next to me is empty, and I am at peace. But wait a minute ... the bus driver, Fred, has just told us that his cell phone is out, and there are a few indicator lights coming on speaking of possible troubles with the bus. We will have to stop so he can call back to the terminal—my first delay? But I am still at peace because the trip is in the hands of somebody bigger than Fred—the One sitting beside me in the empty seat!

Fred has been told to press on to Portland where we will change buses. We have just passed Waterville and are heading to Augusta. It has been such a pleasant ride so far that I am beginning to believe the Good Lord has simply given me a day off to meditate, pray, and read my Bible uninterrupted. Just imagine a heavenly Father who sends you on a rescue mission, only to discover that you are the one being rescued! Rescued from a busy church schedule of counseling, camp work, and correspondence. I was supposed to be ministering to ninety kids this week in Canada, but instead I am alone on a bus with Jesus as my traveling companion heading for Europe! The empty seat isn't really empty after all. All I can think of is that Jesus has done to me what he did for His disciples when He said:

> Come ye yourselves apart ... and rest awhile: for there were many coming and going and they had no leisure so much as to eat. (Mark 6:31)

I sit amazed that my Savior arranged it so that on the first leg of my journey, it is just Him and me from Bangor to Portland. I must admit I am singing as I travel and the tune on my heart and the words on my lips are from the pen of Ira F. Stanphill:

## Come Apart

I traveled alone upon this lonesome way, my burdens are heavy and dark is my day. I looked for a friend not knowing that He had all of the time been looking for me. The road may be long to heaven's pearly gate. I know that it's narrow I know that it's straight. But Jesus is there through eternity, we'll travel along just Jesus and me. Now it is Jesus and me for each tomorrow, for every heartache and every sorrow. I know that I can depend upon my new found Friend; and so the end it is Jesus and me.

# 4

## I'll Meet You in Paris

My last words to Marnie on the phone, were, "I'll meet you in Paris!" My missionary minded daughter was on her second short-term mission's trip to Africa in four years when she picked up malaria. It was a mild case, and within a week she had recovered. However, with only ten days to go before returning home, she contracted a parasite from either infected food or polluted water in a village in Togo. The result was a quick trip to a mission hospital and thirty hours on an IV to get her fluid levels stable. It also took plenty of medicine to get rid of the persistent parasite. Weak and very sick, Marnie struggled against the timetable that would get her home in time to start her senior year at Lancaster Bible College in Pennsylvania.

It took three days to get her eating again, but with each passing hour her strength seemed to improve. Nevertheless, the thought arose that I might have to travel to Africa to bring her home. The obstacles seemed impossible! I hadn't used my passport in twenty-nine years; to renew it would surely take more than the few days we had? Then we would need to figure out the logistics of getting in and out of Africa on the same plane, which seemed impossible as well? And I was supposed to be starting a week of camp meetings in Canada the very day I need to go get her; not to mention the unexpected, unplanned cost of the trip? Could it be done? But does not the Bible say?

FOR WITH GOD NOTHING SHALL BE IMPOSSIBLE!
(Luke 1:37)

Almost from the first moment of conception, God began to work in marvelous ways. First, the passport. The lady at the Ellsworth post office went out of her way to get my old passport to Boston within hours of my request after I told her my story. In three days, I had my new passport in hand. I never thought the government could work so fast! Second, the tickets. Our travel agent quickly worked out a schedule of buses and planes that would get me to Paris one hour after Marnie arrived from Togo. The flight from Lome was full, so Marnie and I would have to rendezvous in Paris, our closest connection. Third, the camp meeting. I called my good friend, Dwayne Gray, and within two hours he was able to switch my week with that of another man, Dale Gallagher. He would take my week, and I would take his. Dale told Dwayne that he had wondered why he'd kept that week open! Fourth, the money. Over the few days before I left, over half of the money for the trip had come in. (The total cost of the trip was $1,800, and before the bills came due, the Lord sent over $2,100!)

As I write this down, I am at peace that the Master Travel Agent has it all mapped out, and that He has not only been guiding my steps, but that He has a purpose for it all. For one thing, He has shown me:

> Faithful is He that calleth you, who also will do it.
> (1 Thessalonians 5:24)

I have also learned that though He sometimes works slowly, that doesn't mean He can't work quickly when needs be. We must be ready at a moment's notice to go when he says go, even if that means, "I'll meet you in Paris!"

## 5

## A Letter to Co

Dear Co (my nickname for my wife, Coleen),

I am planning to return with our daughter as I write you on this bus to Boston, but just in case this trip takes me to another rendezvous, I wanted you to have this letter. (Our son's call last night got me to thinking of what I would do if my trans-Atlantic flight crashed!)

Among the memories of bygone years (thirty-two for us now), there still shines a beautiful life I fell in love with in high school. I can honestly say I am so blessed! We've certainly had our ups and downs, but through them all these thing have remained—our love for God, for each other, and for our children (the reason I am on this bus heading for Paris!). I know I don't need to write this, but as I said, just in case the Good Lord has another plan for me, I want you to hear these things once more from me, if only by way of this letter. It seems I have always been able to express myself better in written form than verbally.

I first want to thank you for who you are and what you are. I have never had occasion to doubt you, be ashamed of you, or question your love for me. I have never lost my trust of you, and your integrity is still in tact after three decades. I thank you for giving me a home, making me a home, and being a homemaker instead of a career wife. I still marvel at your self-sacrifice for our children and me. For all those years, we were first in your life and you were last; even behind the church. Thanks for all the prayers and all the times you put my clothes out. At times I know you were more of a maid than wife, more servant than lover, more scrubwoman than lady of the manse (parsonage). As I looked out the bus window to watch you drive off to our lives in Ellsworth, I must admit I thought what if that was our last prayer, our last hug, our last kiss together? If it was, I am still blessed!

The bus is rolling on south to Portland as I ponder my future, and I have just a few things for you to continue to do for me, if you will. Keep praying for our son, as I am doing now and will to the end. If I don't get to Marnie, I know she will make it home without me; give her a big hug and tell her, "Bubby (Marnie's name for me) loved you and was on his way to get you." Tell the people at church, "I have finished the course" (2 Timothy 4:7). Tell my folks "I kept the faith," and may it be known that "I fought the good fight to the end." I'm thinking now of how you always were there when I came home—you're smiling face and marvelous sandwiches. I know I haven't said it enough, or told you enough, but I do love you with all of my heart and soul. There are many more curves left on this trip, and I don't know if I will make them all, but if I do, I'm sure you'll be there when I get off the plane, hand in hand with your "rose!" Till we meet in Bangor, or by our tree (you know the one with the pink roses) near the river of God.

In HIS Service Together,
Bear (Coleen's nickname for me)

## 6

## From Portland to Philly

I'M AT GATE 20 in the USAir terminal in Boston, about ready to board an early flight to Philly. I was supposed to leave at 2:45 p.m., but now I'm leaving an hour earlier. Portland to Philly is the second-longest part of my trip; Philly to Paris will be the longest. So far so good! We lost a bit of time because of bus troubles in Maine and traffic in Boston, but it appears I will be ahead of schedule by the time I get to Philadelphia.

Fred, the bus driver, was very polite, as were the ticket agents at Logan Airport. I had a chance to share my story with them, and they seemed genuinely concerned and helpful. I must admit, I have been very surprised as I go into the 7th hour of this most extraordinary trip; a trip 10 days ago I never dreamed I would take. But my heavenly Father has shown Himself faithful and amazingly true once again!

I am now traveling with "Jeremiah 33:3 peace":

> Call unto me, and I will answer thee, and shew thee great and mighty things, which thou knowest not.

My only distraction to this point was a few glimpses of Alfred Hitchcock's suspense thriller, "Rear Window," that I watched on the bus from Portland to Boston. Despite the occasional glance, I have kept my mind stayed on Him.

> Thou wilt keep him in perfect peace, whose mind is stayed on thee: because he trusteth in Thee. (Isaiah 26:3)

I am still trying to reason why I am actually going on this pilgrimage to Paris. Marnie's last email showed her better, but the door opened and the pathway cleared, so I am following my Savior and Guide. He has gotten me to Boston on time; now I am off to Philly.

I suspect this is how it will be for our rendezvous in the sky (1 Thessalonians 4:13–17) with Christ, another journey I will take one day. If it is anything like this trip, then I expect it will be a pleasant ride and a clear flight. The sky has been blue and the air warm, all the way from Bangor. I have traveled in comfort, and I can't get over what a relaxed time I've had. The companionship has been sweet and the conversation thrilling. Like Hitchcock's character in "Rear Window," I've had time to sit back and get a good look at what has been going on around me. In my busy life, I don't take time very often to enjoy the ride, taken in the sights, and "smell the roses"!

I am rejoicing in this newfound traveling peace. I am not a traveler by nature, especially when I have to trust the driving to others. Yet I have discovered on this mission that I can say, and sing with Fanny Crosby:

> All the way my Savior leads me, what have I to ask beside? Can I doubt His tender mercy, who thro' life has been my Guide?

Whether Portland to Philly, or home to heaven, I'm at peace!

# 7

# What Is Man?

I AM FLYING DOWN the Atlantic coast of America to Philly as I write these thoughts on USAir flight #732. I am winging my way south so that I might fly east. I am ultimately heading for Paris to rendezvous with my daughter, who is on her way "out of Africa." As I look out the window, I am amazed again at the smallness of man and his world at 20,000 feet. I am reminded again just how tiny are his boats and his beachfront property from high above the clouds. The plane I am on is still big, but as we fly quietly above the earth and all its happenings, I can only say with the psalmist:

> O Lord our Lord, how excellent is thy name in all the earth! Who hast set thy glory above the heavens ... when I consider thy heavens, the works of thy fingers ... which thou hast ordained: what is man, that thou art mindful of him? and the son of man, that thou visitest him? (Psalms 8:1, 3–4)

Every once in a while the average human being needs to see his world from God's vantage point. We can't get very high compared to God, but now at 28,000 feet, it is just as good. It was the great Hebrew prophet Isaiah, who said, "Thus saith the Lord, The heaven is my throne, and the earth is my footstool" (Isaiah 66:1). From this height, it even appears that I could place my feet on one of the many islands that have passed below me. If my world looks that small to me, and I am only in the first heaven (Genesis 1:8), what must God see from the third heaven (2 Corinthians 12:2)?

This trip to Paris has once again brought me face to face with my frailty and His superiority. I see clearly now that to look down from this flying machine can be very depressing, but to look up is glorifying. During the early days of the Pacific War, a young American flyer by the name of John G. Magee Jr., wrote a poem called, "High Flight." Flying for the Royal Canadian Air Force, Magee died in aerial combat on December 11, 1941, just four days after Pearl Harbor. His poem and its inspiration have outlived him:

> Oh! I have slipped the surly bonds of earth and danced the skies on laughter-silvered wings; sunward I've climbed, and joined the tumbling mirth of sun-spit clouds—and done a hundred things you have not dreamed of—wheeled and soared and swung high in the sunlit silence. Hov'ring there I've chased the shouting wind along and flung my eager craft through footless halls of air. Up, up the long, delirious burning blue I've topped the wind—swept heights with easy grace where never lark, nor even eagle flew—and, while with silent lifting mind I've trod the high untrespassed sanctity of space, put out my hand and touched the face of God!

What is man? God created man to hold His hand and walk and talk with Him and yes, to touch His face, as I have today, from my 28,000-foot seat!

# 8

## All Routes Lead to Paris

I HAVE FLOWN THE Pacific Ocean from Los Angeles to Sydney, Australia, but that was in 1972. I am now following a route that will take me across the Atlantic Ocean twice in twenty-four hours. I have never been to Paris, or on the road to Paris, yet it seems that all routes do lead to Paris. I have already traveled from my home in Ellsworth to Bangor to Boston and soon to Philadelphia. So before heading east, I must travel south. The road has already been seven hours long, yet they have been pleasant miles, this route to Paris. The traveling has been quiet and peaceful and so have the travelers. I have spent the bulk of my time talking to my heavenly Father, hearing Him clearly and writing down the messages He has wanted me to record. This one has to do with the route to Heaven, compared to the road to Paris.

Along my route today, I could have made many a detour to just about any place on this planet. As I write, I am on a plane heading for Philly that will then go on to Detroit. I will leave this plane in a few minutes because it will not take me to Paris, where my daughter, Marnie, is waiting for me. It is sad to me that so many of my traveling companions to Heaven have decided to depart (1 Timothy 4:1) and fall away (2 Thessalonians 2:3) on this trip we are taking together to "glory." They, like Demas, (2 Timothy 4:10) have been attracted to signs that say "New York" or "Washington." I have kept my eyes on only those signs that point me to my final destination. I like what Vance Havner wrote for a spiritual application to this fatal flaw of many a man:

> A book on missions says that the early apostles may have been mistaken when they insisted that there is no other name but Christ whereby we must be saved (Acts 4:12). Such exclusiveness, we are told, does not make for dialogue. Why should it? There is nothing to dialogue about. If no man comes to God but by Jesus Christ that settles it! Why get out new maps offering a selection of highways when all others are ways that seem right unto a man but end in death?

I have my route, and I have my travel agenda for this trip to Paris. Why would I go any other place? Marnie will only be at the end of this route to Paris. The same is true of my heavenly journey. Why would I want to end this trip anyplace but where I will see my Savior "face to face"? As for me, I will only take the route that leads to Paris on this trip and Heaven on the next. Vance offers this advice about heavenly "guidance" on the path to Heaven:

> Guidance; "in all thy ways acknowledge Him and He shall direct thy path." It is easier to preach about guidance than to be sure of it in some cases. Sometimes we expect the Lord to make it plainer than He does. By the Word, prayer, meditation, circumstance, sometimes the advice of true Christian friends, by steps and by stops. "God leads His dear children along."

Follow Him and Him alone to Heaven!

## 9

## Philadelphia

From a lofty USAir jet I view Philadelphia. "And to the angel of the church of Philadelphia write . . ." (Revelation 3:7). I know this verse is speaking of the Biblical Philadelphia, not the American Philadelphia, but both mean the same thing—brotherly love!

I have never flown into Philly's airport before, and though I have visited downtown Philadelphia, you can't get a good perspective of the size of the city until you see it from above. As I gazed down on the city of brotherly love, these verses from the pen of Paul began to flood my mind:

> Be kindly affectioned one to another with brotherly love. (Romans 12:10)

> But as touching brotherly love ye need not that I write unto you: ye yourselves
> Are taught of God to love one another.
> (1 Thessalonians 4:9)

> Let brotherly love continue. (Hebrews 13:2)

Whether a Christian or a city, the Good Lord would have brotherly love abounding!

I was stirred by this thought on my way to Paris by way of Philadelphia. Marnie, my daughter, waits for me at the end of my next flight. She might call it "Bubby love," not brotherly love, but no matter what it is called, it's the reason I am on this plane to Philly. Despite being twenty-one and a college senior, she still uses that name for me, and it defines the love we have for each other. It was the first name she called me when she was but a baby in my arms, and nobody else calls me by that special name. I am on this trip because I am her earthly father, and she is on this trip because she was following the call of her heavenly Father. Some may call it a waste, but I see it as a grand opportunity to show my daughter just how much I love her, not just as a daughter, but also as a sister in Christ. Brotherly love is the love that happens between the Disciples of Christ!

We are both in the service of the King. That service for her began seventeen years ago; mine forty-three years. Our first service together took place in the nursing homes of Aroostook County, Maine. Over nearly two decades, Marnie has served the Lord in Awana, children's church, two summers as a Child Evangelism Fellowship missionary to Downeast Maine, and two summers in Africa. She has also worked in three of the four churches I have pastored, as well as being a resident assistant at Lancaster Bible College. Whether together or separated, we have labored in His work in brotherly love.

So as I fly high over Philadelphia, I am reminded of why I am rendezvousing in Paris. I am motivated by my love as a father, as a co-worker, and as a brother in Christ. Paul commanded:

> I commend unto you Phoebe (Marnie), our sister ...that ye assist her in whatsoever business she hath need of you. (Romans 16:1–2)

I go to Paris to be of any assistance I can be to a great servant of Christ because of brotherly love!

## 10

## The View from a Window

I HAVE LOOKED OUT many a window on this day of travel. I am on a private mission to rendezvous with my daughter in France. I promised her when she left for her second short-term mission trip to Africa that if trouble came her way, I would find her where she was. If everything falls into place, I will find her at Terminal #1 at the Charles De Gaulle Aero port outside Paris early tomorrow morning. Until then, I have a few more windows to look out!

Very early this morning I looked out my bedroom window in Ellsworth, Maine, to a beautiful summer morning after a night's shower. The world smelled fresh and cool as a new coastal day began. The birds were singing as the residents of our little city came alive. Within the hour, I was looking out the window of my wife's car as she drove me to Bangor and the Concord Trail ways Terminal on Union Street. The traffic was light and the air refreshing and I left the window down the entire trip. Around 8:20 a.m., I waved goodbye to my dear wife through the window of the bus. I was amazed to see no tears. After a loving hug, I was on my way, on a quest that had been approved by my earthly wife and my heavenly Father. The view from the window was very clear as I settled back for a four-and-a-half hour bus ride to Logan Airport in Boston.

I watched Maine disappear through that same window and another one like it as we switched buses in Portland. Once in Boston, I only had to look out the terminal window for less than an hour before I was looking out my first airplane window of the day. Through that window I saw only white clouds, blue seas, green land, and brown islands as I winged my way from Logan to Philly. It was a smooth and safe flight that brought me to the windows I now gaze out. The windows before me look out onto the huge runways at Philadelphia International Airport. I see nothing but big terminals and long taxiways. This picture window certainly tells where I am and where I am heading. The plane I will be flying to Paris on is already outside this window, but I have a few more hours to wait until I can look out its windows.

As I wait for my boarding call, I take time to look through another window—the window of God's Word. I've had time today to read from Revelation 18 to Psalms 31. I am reading an old orange Gideon New Testament given to me many years ago by a good Gideon friend and church deacon, Joe Gover. Most Gideon New Testaments have Psalms and Proverbs after the Book of the Revelation. With so much time on my hands, I am exhorted by Paul:

> Till I come, give attendance to reading.
> (1 Timothy 4:13)

From where I have been sitting, I have been able to view the end of the age through "the window of the Word." As with the windows so far on this trip, the Biblical window is very clear about what is going to take place in the last days. Oh, that more people might take the time to prepare for their future trip, for as sure as I will finish my course to Paris and back, so too will this world finish its course, but for most there will be no coming back!

11

## Marvelous Machines

From Gate A7 at the USAir International Terminal in Philadelphia, I watch the marvelous machines of the air coming and going as I wait to board my flight to Paris. Everywhere I behold the miracle of flying. I have just walked from Gate C31 to A7 through crowds of people heading in every direction on the compass. The thriving throng moves about, putting in their time, as I am, before the next flight out. Some shop, some stop to eat, and others like me are sitting and waiting, pondering how far we have come and how far we still have to travel. For me, I am in my nineth hour of this odyssey to rendezvous with my daughter in Paris.

What some call "the melting pot of society," I sense is more like "the pressure cooker of society!" I have just flown from Boston to Philly with a continuous traveler, a businessman from Morgantown, Pennsylvania, who is heading home for three days before he is off again to who knows where? My trip has been so far a wonderful adventure, but for my seatmate on the last flight, it is nothing but a job. Anyone who is sitting where I am this afternoon can't help but be moved by the invention of man. Orville and Wilbur Wright would be proud of how far we Americans have come since they taught us to fly. However, there is one thing, despite the years, that we are still having trouble with: patience in flying.

Man has yet to invent a machine that will help us be patient. What a marvelous machine that would be! As I have observed on this trip, it is these marvelous machines of flight that have made us more impatient than ever. Perhaps it is because with these machines, we have learned to expect things to happen more quickly than they should. All I know is that I am practicing on this trip:

> Be patient therefore, brethren, unto the coming of the Lord. Behold, the husbandman waiteth for the precious fruit of the earth, and hath patience for it, until he receive the early and the latter rain. (James 5:7)

Only God could have put this trip together, and only God can pull off the timing of my meeting with my daughter in Paris! He set it up, He set the schedule, and He will get me there on time. So I will be patient for the early or latter flight, and I will wait on the Lord until He brings me to the fruit I am looking for in this harvest: my precious Marnie Lee!

What has impressed me so far on this journey is just how calm I have been. If there is something I hate, it is traveling and not knowing where I am. I have never been where I am now, and I certainly have never been where I am going next. Yet I don't feel lost. I have this perfect peace that I will find Marnie at the Charles de Gaulle Aero port, and we will by God's grace find out way home again. What started out 9 days ago as an impossibility has turned into a possibility through the miracle of this marvelous machine we call an airplane. Another age or another time, I could never have hoped to meet my daughter in Paris in just 19 hours. And if God can pull off a trip to Paris, He will one day pull off a trip to Paradise without the aid of any marvelous machines (Hebrews 11:5).

## 12

## To Sit and Think

I HAVE TRAVELED ALL the way to Philadelphia to sit and think. I don't get much time at home to sit and think. With ministry obligations and family responsibilities, my mind is more often than not busy thinking on what I must do next. One of the side blessings on this trip is the time I have had just to sit and think. Since 8 a.m. this morning until now (it is nearing 5 p.m.), I have done a lot of sitting and thinking.

As I write these observations I am sitting again. I am in the Philadelphia International Airport waiting to board my overseas flight to Paris. The line to the ticket counter is very long, so I thought I would sit and think a bit more before I check in. As I have done off and on throughout this day, my sitting and thinking has been on God's Word, and particularly the Book of Psalms.

I love to meditate, and God loves for us to meditate. "This book of the law shall not depart out of thy mouth; but thou shalt meditate therein day and night" (Joshua 1:8). As I've had all day, I am also going to have all night to ponder the precepts of God's Holy Word. I started this morning with the first Psalm, and I read in Psalms 1:2:

> But his delight is in the law of the Lord; and in his law doth he meditate day and night.

Time is the key factor when it comes to chewing the spiritual "cud." I used to watch my father's cows on our dairy farm in northern Maine wasting their time chewing the cud, but now I crave time simply to sit and think and chew! I met a man on my bus trip from Portland to Boston who was on his way to a three-day conference in New York. He said he was looking forward to the time away because it gave him time to think. Mostly everybody else was listening to music or watching the onboard movie, but this man spent three hours thinking about public sculptures, his passion. If he can spend that amount of time on the abstract, I certainly can spend that much time on the Almighty.

Let us be honest. Most people want a distraction so they don't have to think. Rebuked by the passion of the man in the next seat, I spent my time writing and reading, and guess what I found. As I began to read the Psalms in Biblical order, something I have done often, I was struck this time by a recurring theme I had never noticed before:

> Blessed are all they that put their trust in him. (Psalms 2:12)
>
> O Lord my God in thee do I put my trust. (Psalms 7:1)
>
> In the Lord put I my trust. (Psalms 11:1)
>
> O God, for in thee do I put my trust. (Psalms 16:1)
>
> In whom I will trust. (Psalms 18:2)
>
> O my God, I trust in thee. (Psalms 25:2)
>
> For I put my trust in thee. (Psalms 25:20)
>
> I have trusted also in the Lord. (Psalms 26:1)
>
> In thee, O Lord, do I put my trust? (Psalms 31:1)

Do you think the Lord was trying to tell me something?

## 13

## Delayed Flight

My trip to rendezvous with my daughter in Paris had gone off without a hitch until Flight #26. Fred, the Concord Trailways bus driver, got me to Boston just a few minutes behind schedule, but that was made up for when I was able to get on an early flight to Philadelphia. With an extra hour and a half in hand, I thought I was doing great. I even boarded my plane for Paris on time, but then the gridlock on the runway caught up with my fellow passengers and me.

As I sit patiently in seat 33D, I ponder another delayed flight I am involved in. My Lord, Jesus Christ, promised a "flight home" to His Church almost two millennia ago. We Baptists call it the rapture, while others call it a translation, but in reality it will be a flight—in rapture or in death. There are some old words (written by Albert E. Brumley) to a song I am singing to myself (Ephesians 5:19) as I write these lines:

> Some glad morning when this life is o'er, I'll fly away. To a home on God's celestial shore, I'll fly away. When the shadows of this life have gone, I'll fly away. Like a bird from prison bars has flown, I'll fly away. Just a few more weary days and then, I'll fly away. To a land where joys shall never end, I'll fly

away. I'll fly away, O glory, I'll fly away. When I die hallelujah, by and by, I'll fly away!

Wouldn't it be wonderful if it was from Flight #26, for instead of meeting my daughter in Paris, I would be meeting her in the clouds with our Lord and the rest of our family!

The pen of the Apostle Paul wrote this about our upcoming flight:

> For the Lord himself shall descend from heaven with a shout, with the voice of the archangel, and with the trump of God: and the dead in Christ shall rise first: then we which are alive and remain shall be caught up together with them in the clouds, to meet the Lord in the air: and so shall we ever be with the Lord. (I Thessalonians 4:16–17)

For whatever reason, the Captain of that flight has delayed my departure and that of my fellow Christians. I have been of recent years pondering just why? Is it because the stage is not yet quite set for the appearing of the Anti-Christ (2 Thessalonians 2:8)? Is it because the Church hasn't finished its great commission (Matthew 28:19–20)? Is it because Christ hasn't gotten our place in heaven ready yet (John 14:3)? Or, could it be that I haven't yet finished my course (2 Timothy 4:7)?

I don't know the reason for my delayed flight to Paris, but I am content that like my other Captain (Hebrews 2:10), this captain knows best. If the captain of a mighty airliner knows best when to delay and when to depart, then so does my heavenly Pilot. I will wait and watch and continue to work, because I know that before too long, a call will come that the way is clear and our flight will begin. When the time is right, it will be "up, up, and away," and we won't be traveling in "a beautiful balloon"!

## 14

## Stranger in Service

TODAY I SENSE AGAIN what it feels like to be a stranger (1 Peter 2:11) in "this present world." I prayed the prayer of Jabez (1 Chronicles 4:10) recently, not realizing the Lord would actually enlarge my border all the way to Paris!

I am a homebody that cares neither for travel or timetables. I am content in my little corner of Maine, but the Lord thought it was time for me to get out of my comfort zone, so He has me on my way to Paris to rendezvous with my daughter. This is no vacation, for I will be back in Ellsworth in twenty-eight hours. I'm doing this because of my vocation. I have been a servant of the King of Kings for over forty years, and if He wants me in Paris, then to Paris I will go. He has worked out the details over the last few days so that I might also accomplish a parental obligation. I'm on my way to meet Marnie and to fulfill a promise I made to her mother. As I journey, I am discovering just how much of a stranger and pilgrim I really am in this world.

I am stuck on a runway at the Philadelphia International Airport, waiting to depart for France. The captain of this big bird has just announced that there is a flock of birds (planes) in front of us which will delay our takeoff about an hour. Marnie is in the air, I hope, so the timing of our meeting is now in the hands of the Good Lord. Whatever—He has all schedules in His control, so as a stranger and pilgrim in a foreign plane, I must trust Him.

I am sitting in a middle seat, in the middle row, at the back end of this plane. I am between a horse buyer from Canada and a young French travel agent from Paris. I have been on the road or in the air for twelve hours now. (I left my home on the coast of Maine at 6:50 a.m. and am now in Philadelphia at 6:50 p.m.) I have traveled with scores of people and walked by and through many hundreds more. I haven't seen a familiar face yet in the crowds or with my companions on this trip, and I don't expect to see one until I see my daughter's lovely smile at the end of this flight.

What this trip has reminded me of is the reality of the few familiar faces we see on our pilgrimage here on earth. Today I have only seen a fraction of the billions of people I live on this planet with. We are all strangers, as He was. Jesus came to be "the stranger of Galilee!" What He must have felt when after thirty-three years away from home He finally saw His Father's familiar face. I will be honest. It has only been forty-four days, but I can't wait to see Marnie's face, or her mine. Granted, we will be strangers and pilgrims in Paris, but we will be face to face, and that will be enough. I can't wait until I return from this trip and see only familiar faces again. I believe that's how it will be when we get to Heaven:

> No more strangers and foreigners, but fellow-citizens with the saints, and of the household of God. (Ephesians 2:19)

## 15

## Trusting the Pilot

As I boarded the plane for Paris, I placed myself into the hands of the captain and his crew, trusting they would provide a safe trip to the Charles de Gaulle Aero port. I don't know him or any of his staff. I have never flown on this particular plane before, but I find myself with no worries or fears. I am confident that my pilot has been briefed about any possible problems ahead, as well as any weather conditions that might pop up on our six-and-a-half hour flight across the Atlantic Ocean. I know the captain is in constant contact with the air traffic controllers, and if there is a problem, we will be rerouted around it. I am relaxed and waiting patiently as we near the end of our hour delay on the runway in Philadelphia. My first trans-Atlantic flight and my first trip to Europe are about ready to begin.

During my flight down from Boston, I only felt air turbulence a few times. I think the seat belt light only came on twice. I did feel the plane bounce slightly, but nothing to worry about or to disturb my reading or writing. Looking out the side window I saw many clouds below, but very few at the 28,000-foot level we were traveling. I was confident then, and I am confident now, that my flight to Paris will be the same. I look around and see in the faces of my fellow passengers the same unconcerned look. We all are expecting a smooth, uneventful flight to France.

So why is it we don't put as much trust in our Heavenly Pilot? He too has been briefed on what lies ahead. He has traveled the route before us (John 3:13), and He knows the best paths through the skies of life. I don't know the route to Paris, but the pilot does. So too does Jesus know the way to Heaven, because He is the Way (John 14:6). Instead of sitting back and enjoying the ride of life, I spend so much time trying to guess, predict, and surmise what is going to happen next. Like this trip to Paris to rendezvous with my daughter, I need to trust life's Pilot more and sing with Edward Hooper:

> Jesus, Savior, pilot me over life's tempestuous sea; unknown waves before me roll, hiding rock and treacherous shoal; chart and compass came from Thee: Jesus, Savior, pilot me.

I know on my flight to Paris I may be flying over a "tempestuous sea," not on it, but the practice of trust is the same!

I am determined after this experience to take to heart Peter's exhortation to "... commit the keeping of (my) their souls (soul) to him in well doing, as unto a faithful Creator" (1 Peter 4:19). Oh, that I can put as much confidence in my known Pilot as I have put in this unknown pilot, for "... He knoweth the way that I take ..." (Job 23:10).

Dear Lord, may I be fearless and fretless in the upcoming flights of my life as I have been on this trip. May I show you the same respect and confidence, and more, as I have in this flight's pilot? In Jesus' name. Amen and Amen.

## 16

## One Ocean, One God

It wasn't until I read this by Phillip Keller that I learned of the oneness of the ocean, and as I wing my way across the Atlantic Ocean to rendezvous with my daughter in Paris I have a better idea what Keller meant when he wrote:

> There are some aspects of the ocean that 20th century technology has opened up to our understanding with tremendous interest. One of these great discoveries is that all the water of all the oceans is in fact one gigantic fluid. It is in constant motion and movement, circulating by means of colossal currents from pole to pole and clear around the earth. The ancient idea that each ocean or great inland sea, such as the Mediterranean, was more or less a self-contained body of water, restricted roughly within its own continental basin and boundaries, is no longer valid. We now know for a fact that these great oceans actually flow into one another in gigantic subsurface rivers that make the Mississippi, Nile, or Amazon seems like mere trickles in comparison.

This has helped me to understand why so often in Scripture, the sea is mentioned, not "the seas": ". . . that had the waters round about it, whose rampart was the sea, and her wall was from the sea?" (Nahum 3:8).

Nahum in his comparison above is contrasting Nineveh with the Nile and Egypt, but in his analogy, he speaks of rivers and waters, but not of seas. It is the sea! The Psalmist says, "He gathereth the waters of the sea together as a heap ..." (Psalms 33:7). Note again, plural waters, but singular sea. I have checked numerous verses and this concept is clearly seen throughout the Bible. Interestingly, another scientific reality long taught in God's Word is just beginning to gain acceptance in the scientific community. Man has always been slow to accept the Bible at face value, but once again technology and tests have proven the Creator right again.

So what for us could be the meaning of this scientific precept to some spiritual concept? For me, could the one ocean be pointing us to the One God? Man has for so long believed in the plurality of gods. Like the oceans, separate beings interacting, but distinct. The Greeks and the Romans had panoply of gods, and modern man is trying again to join all the gods of the different world religions into one happy family of gods. But Scriptures clearly say:

> Hear, O Israel: the Lord our God is one Lord.
> (Deuteronomy 6:4)

Even in the New Testament, through the pen of Paul, we hear, "One God and Father of all, who is above all, and through all, and in all" (Ephesians 4:6). With one ocean, there is no room for another, and with one God and one Lord, there is no room for others. All talk of other oceans and other gods is nothing but a lie of Satan.

## 17

## 13 Days in October

I AM WINGING MY way eastward toward a rendezvous with my daughter in Paris. It is late and I have been on the road since early this morning. I have already traveled from Bangor, Maine, to Boston, Massachusetts to Philadelphia, Pennsylvania. I am nearly five hours into a 6-and-a-half hour flight across the Atlantic Ocean. I have just taken my first break of the day from reading and writing and praying to watch the movie, "13 Days," about the Cuban Missile Crisis of October 17–30, 1962. It brought back a few memories, as I was but an elementary school kid when the world came very close to blowing itself up. As I watch for the sunrise over the continent, I have a few thoughts about this important event in World history.

History has always spoken of Armageddon (Revelation 16:16). Back at the turn of the last century, President Teddy Roosevelt said, "We stand at Armageddon." He was watching as World War I rolled over the continent I am now flying towards. General Douglas MacArthur said after World War II, "If we do not now devise some more equitable system, Armageddon will be at our door!" Most of us that lived through the Cuban Missile Crisis thought that Armageddon was certainly at the door, yet this world has survived nearly 40 more years since those climactic days in late October 1962. So what is going on, and why have we come so close and yet the Valley of Esdraelon remains a quiet place still today?

As with Israel, Cuba seems like such a small country compared to the United States and Russia, or even the European countries, yet it survived the Bay of Pigs and the Cuban Missile Crisis, and Castro has outlasted eight U.S. presidents! It reminds me of this verse in Daniel 2:21:

> And He changeth the times and the seasons: He removeth kings and setteth up kings ...

Good or bad governments stay in control until the Good Lord says, "Enough is enough." When will we realized that it is the Almighty, not the United Nations or the United States that controls the seats of power in this old world? Oh, the final clash at Megiddo will take place; you can count on that, but not until the Lord calls the nations to judgment. Two world wars, and many minor wars and crises have taught us that the world can't destroy itself, even when it appears to want to!

The final thought I got out of my two hours of reliving history at 32,000 feet is that negotiation, not conflict, eventually settled the Cuban Missile Crisis. But I am as sure about this as anything I believe: in the last days when the Lord does come back, He is not coming back to negotiate! Jesus will return to put his enemies under His feet (Psalms 110:1). History will not end with a crisis diverted or delayed, but it will end in a valley of slaughter so unbelievable that the world wars combined with all other wars will look like the Cuban Missile Crisis in comparison!

## 18

## Joshua's Day

I DID IT! I have just lived through a 'Joshua Day':

> And the sun stood still, and the moon stayed, until the people had avenged themselves upon their enemies. Is not this written in the book of Jasher? So the sun stood still in the midst of heaven, and hasted not to go down about a whole day. (Joshua 10:13)

In the summer of 1972, I missed a day in my life because of the International Dateline. I went to sleep over the Pacific on June 6th and woke up over the coast of Australia on June 8th. I had completely missed June 7, 1972. On my return trip ten weeks later from a short-term mission's trip to Western Australia; my August 18th was thirty-six hours long. As I began my trip to Paris and back in forty hours, I was hoping to not see the sun go down in twenty-four hours. Because Paris is six hours ahead of Maine time, I was hoping to see the sunset and sunrise within hours of each other, about a whole day! I left my home on the coast of Maine just as the sun was rising, about 6:30 a.m., and I was scheduled to fly into France just as the sun was rising on the next day!

The trip so far has been pleasant and warm, but air-conditioned buses, air-conditioned terminals, and air-conditioned planes will make any hot, summer trip comfortable.

I was delayed in my take-off from Philadelphia, but before sunset we took off to chase the last rays of the July sun. As the western light slips away, will we be fast enough to catch the rising rays of the eastern light? It will probably be my last chance to witness what it must have been like on that extraordinary day when God granted Joshua's prayer request (Joshua 10:12) and stopped the heavens in their tracks.

I too have a prayer for this trip, that the Good Lord will go before me and destroy all delays and cancellations. That He will push aside all bottlenecks and bad weather that I might be in Paris within a day to rendezvous with my daughter. I too want a day I have never, ever experienced:

> And there was no day like that day before or after it, that the Lord hearkened unto the voice of a man: for the Lord fought for Israel. (Joshua 10:14)

At 10 p.m. Maine time, or 4 a.m. Paris time, the rays of sunlight faded from the portside windows. It went finally dark on this my extraordinary day, but at nearly six-hundred miles per hour, I was soon seeing the rays from a French sunrise. As I finish these thoughts, it is 6 a.m. Paris time. I am flying into a bright summer sunrise over the continent, and the Lord has answered my prayer. All my enemies have been defeated on this day of battle; fear and doubt and hang-ups have all been slaughtered because of a simple prayer. It has been a carefree trip, and within twenty-four hours of actual time, I have traveled from Ellsworth, Maine, to Paris, France. Like Joshua, I didn't need a full day, but just "about a whole day!"

## 19

## Joy Comes in the Morning

I HAVE TRAVELED ALL day and early into the morning, French time. It is still only 1:30 a.m. in Maine, but I am finally in France, or rather over France. From my window I can see that it is a fine, summer day on the continent, and the pilot has just informed us that the weather is pleasant and cool with the possibility of late day showers. I have taken this unexpected journey, crossing the Atlantic Ocean in under twenty-four hours, for the express purpose of meeting with my daughter in Paris, so that we could and can fly back to the United States together after her extraordinary summer in Africa!

I have been on the road and in the air for eighteen-and-a-half hours as my fellow travelers and I touch down at the Charles de Gaulle Aero port. I will allow most of the other passengers to disembark first because I am in seat 33D of thirty-five rows. As I wait, I will finish my conversation with Hensel Wood, who is a horse-jumping enthusiast from Canada. His wife is a member of the Canadian Olympic Equitation Team, and he is on his way to a series of horse shows in France to buy first-class jumping horses for the team. As we talked off and on throughout the night, I learned a lot about the sport of "the rich and famous."

It was a nice distraction as I waited the final hours before my daughter and I could be reunited.

If everything went according to schedule, Marnie should already be at the airport, as her flight from Lome, Togo, was supposed to have beaten me to France by about an hour. As I get up from my seat and said goodbye to Hensel, I began to think:

> Is Marnie there? What will I do if she isn't? How will I find her in this vast airport?

I am comfortable in the Northern Maine woods, but put me in a world-class city airport and I am lost before I start. A farmer's son from Maine who is only on his second international trip in fifty years isn't prepared for the complications an airport the size of Rhode Island will throw at him! But I promised the "apple of my eye" that I would rendezvous with her in Paris, and no matter the pitfalls and problems, that is what I am determined to do.

As I get off Flight #26, I follow Mr. Wood up the ramp and into the lobby. No Marnie! I can see that we have disembarked at a side terminal, and I know there has to be customs somewhere, so I chase the crowd down a long corridor. I try to keep up with Mr. Wood because at least I can speak his language, but he is in a hurry and soon is far ahead and out of sight. The planeload of about two hunderd passengers has spread out as we enter the main terminal, and there is where I first spot her smiling face. My dear daughter is standing to one side, scanning the departing passengers in search of her "bubby." I spot her before she sees me, and for a moment, all I can think about is this phrase from the Psalmist, and how right he was when he wrote:

> JOY COMETH IN THE MORNING!
> (Psalms 30:5)

## 20

## The Shadow of Your Smile

Joy for me was not found in Paris, France, but in "the shadow of your smile," for "... in thy presence is fullness of joy" (Psalms 16:11).

My dear daughter, when I began recording these memories yesterday morning, I never imagined how much I had missed your smile this summer. Oh, I know you don't think you have a pretty smile, or that you are beautiful, but to me both are true. Why do you think I travel to see you as often as I do? In four years at Bob Jones University, my parents traveled only once to see me; your mother and I have made 10 trips to Lancaster Bible College, and now I have come to France—just to see the sights? No, to see your smile! I don't know how many times your mother said last week, "Wouldn't it be nice just to see Marnie's smiling face?"

I have been pondering over the last few hours "the shadow of your smile," what it is and why it is? The shadow of your smile is the glow of a holy life. As Pascal put it:

> The serene beauty of a holy life is the most powerful influence in the world next to the might of God.

It is through your smile that you have most helped the helpless. Your smile is the radiation of godliness from within being revealed without. It is God's way of smiling on a troubled world through His saint. Smiles are beautiful emblems of the love of God, and they, like gold, cannot perish, because they are stored in the memory of those who have seen "the shadow of your smile," as so many have this summer in Africa!

I still remember your first smile. It was dramatic because you never smiled much as a small child; you were in too much pain to smile (Marnie was born with a birth defect that caused massive infections that dangerously affected her kidneys and bladder. At the tender age of eighteen months Marnie had to have a major operation to correct the defect), but on those odd moments when the infection was under control, I would look into your eyes and you would smile at me. More often than not it was in the dead of night when it was my turn to comfort you through the long, painful hours of darkness. I recall one night when a full moon bathed the room in a wondrous glow that I woke from a nap to find you smiling at me. It was almost as if you said, "Bubby, you rest. I'm feeling fine now!" It is the shadows of those smiles that still make me smile, and yes, shed a tear! I recall the smile after your operation as you raced down the hospital hall with poles in hand to greet me during a late afternoon visit. Those smiles were worth all the affliction and suffering we had endured together for nearly two years!

Now I wait patiently for that next smile—that smile that melts my heart and thrills my soul. As a soft summer breeze on a warm evening, your smile calms a hall of college girls and just about anybody that comes within the sight of your face. It is infectious and inviting, and I am glad that I saw it first. Like the shadows of a past time, your smiles will keep the day bright through the times of separation ahead. So, the next time you're down or discouraged because of distance, just smile and know your father is smiling back, as he did that morning in Paris!

## 21

## African Feet

HER HAIR WAS THE right color—strawberry blonde—as were those brilliant, blue eyes. That inviting smile was there, as was her peaches-and-cream complexion. Yes, that was my Marnie Lee, standing at the end of a very long hall, waiting patiently for her father to disembark from Flight #26 from Philadelphia. But was there something different?

I know now why I had missed it at first. It was because I was looking up, not down, as I hugged the loved one I had traveled over 4,000 miles to rendezvous with. I was more concerned with her health than her appearance after two rough weeks of malaria and a parasite or two. The six weeks in Togo, West Africa, had taken their toll, but in my eyes she looked great, and the hug was worth the nineteen hours it took for me to travel from my home on the coast of Maine to this airport in Europe. We laughed and talked, for she too had seen a change. While Marnie was in Africa, I had cut off my mustache. Marnie had never seen me without one, for I had kept one ever since she was born in 1980. She said that was why she had a hard time picking me out of the crowd. But as for me, it wasn't until we boarded the train for Paris that I had a chance to really look her over from top to bottom, and it was then I saw her "African feet!"

Marnie had spent forty-four days in West Africa proclaiming the good news of Jesus Christ. The country of Togo was hot and dusty, so she spent her summer in flip-flops; her many miles of walking through the villages and market places had taken a toll on her feet. The highways and hedges, paths and trails, were rough and rugged. Her toes, big and small, had been exposed to all forms of punishment and disease, and as we rode the train into the city, I could see the marks and scars of taking the Gospel to the bush country of Africa. As I gazed upon those "African feet," I understood for the first time Paul's proclamation of Isaiah 52:7:

> How beautiful are the feet of them that preach the gospel of peace, and bring glad tidings of good things! (Romans 10:15)

On that ride into Paris, I came to the realization that God chooses His prophets not by their intellect or their outward appearance or personal skills, but by their feet. In a day where letters and degrees are primary, we have forgotten the importance of feet! The GO is still in the GOspel, and it takes feet like my daughter's to go to the far off and distant places where no television or radio has yet arrived. What good are all the modern gadgets if there is no "GO" in them? I know now why God chose the people He did to do his work in difficult areas of the world; they all had great feet—Taylor, Chinese feet; Carey, Indian feet; Livingstone, African feet, to name but a few special feet of Church history.

In a world that sends its talent scouts out looking for the wrong characteristics, we need to review who and what we are looking for in a servant. Our first question ought to be:

> Do they have the right feet for the job?

## 22

## A Piece of Our Heart

As my daughter and I talked on the train into Paris of her adventures in Africa, I was listening for the answer to the question she had gone to Africa to ask. Marnie had been to Africa between her junior and senior years of high school, but she came home wondering if the Almighty was calling her to the "dark continent" to be a missionary. She had returned between her junior and senior years of college to settle the question once and for all. She wanted to know if after her senior year at Lancaster Bible College, was she to make plans for living and ministering in Africa?

My first questions, however, had to do with her health. She had a rough last two weeks with the diseases of Togo, but during that time of illness, she had a great chance to review what she had learned about the outback of Africa and her own abilities and calling. Despite loving the kids and the people and being able to do the work, she had gotten the message that Africa wasn't going to be her final field of service for the King. The Lord told her that He would find others to finish the works she had visited. The great commission would fill the void, and she was to return to Lancaster and wait for her next assignment. Despite the peace of mind in her voice, I did sense a bit of sadness in her heart. I knew what she was feeling, for twenty-nine years before, on another flight across a great ocean; I too felt the pangs of being called away from where my heart longed to serve.

In the summer of 1972, between my junior and senior years at Bob Jones University, I was in Western Australia working with the Aboriginal people of the Gibson Desert. I had gone to the country to confirm what I thought was God's calling to be a missionary. But instead of confirming, the Lord shut the door. It was these words in Ezekiel that cancelled my plans:

> And he said unto me, Son of Man, go, get thee unto the house of Israel (back home to New England), and speak with my words unto them. For thou art not send to a people of a strange speech and of a hard language (the Aboriginals of Australia), but to the house of Israel; not to many people of a strange speech and a hard language, whose words thou canst not understand. Surely, had I sent thee to them, they would have hearkened unto thee. (Ezekiel 3:4–6)

Since that day, I have lived with a small piece of my heart missing. It is hard to leave a part of your heart in a land that was your "first love" evangelically. I could hear in my daughter's voice and see in her eyes that she too had buried a piece of her heart in Africa. Is this why I came to Paris, to help in a funeral service?

Those of us who have loved one people, but have been called to another, know we can't bury our entire heart. We need some for those we will minister to in the future. I've had plenty of heart for the four churches I have pastored over the last thirty years since Australia. I haven't looked back, and I don't intend to go back, but every once in a while I wonder what it would have been like to minister to a people with "a strange speech" that would have listened to me?

## 23

## Charles de Gaulle Airport to Champ de Mars Tour Eiffel

IT HAS BEEN FAIRLY well publicized that the Eiffel Tower in Paris is the number one sightseeing stop when in France. It is not a good place for writing, yet I must write. As my daughter and I roll into Paris from the airport, I have some unsavory and unflattering observations to make about one of the world's showcase cities.

When you move from the quiet countryside of rural France to the pomp and pageantry of downtown Paris, the two views of this European city bring to a stark contrast what is and what isn't. I was impressed, but unmoved, by the cathedrals and chapels of this city. I knew of their deadness and dampness to the Gospel of Jesus Christ. Romanism had taken over and there is hardly any authentic Christianity in this city, except for a hidden remnant. Marnie and I were like Paul and Peter wandering the streets of Rome in their last moments: strangers and pilgrims in a distant land, only awaiting the call home. All along our route from the airport to the Eiffel Tower, we saw the hustle and bustle of a busy people, and all I heard in my ears was the tramp, tramp, tramp of feet heading for Hell's gate at an ever-increasing pace. I could not speak their language either vocally or spiritually, even though France considers itself the Christian land of Joan of Arc! Yet I saw in their dark impressive monuments a trust in fairy tales and figurines as their way to eternal salvation.

Marnie and I spent most of our time in the catacombs of this mighty metropolis—its subway system—but all we saw were people heading nowhere to return somewhere after their day's work was done. We met materialism alive and well in Paris; I thought it was just an American plague! This blight jumped out at us from every café, street vendor, and local artist. I saw nothing that would make me believe that we were not in some pagan village in Northern Togo. Mausoleums or mud, what is the difference when both places know nothing about "the light of the world"? (John 9:5). Can you imagine riding and walking through a huge city known for its lights and not once feeling "the light of the world" except in your own heart, or seeing "the light of the world" except on the face of your traveling companion?

Vance Havner once wrote, "We are too easily impressed by the phony grandeur of our time!" Is Paris impressive? Yes, if you are talking of granite buildings, beautiful parks, and wall-to-wall people. I don't know what I expected to see as I traveled from the terminal to the tower, but I didn't expect I would be as unmoved as I was. Perhaps it was because of why I was there. Perhaps it was because I hadn't slept in twenty-four hours. It could have been a number of things, but one thing was clear:

> A grand place holds no grandeur without God!

## 24

## Ice Cream at the Eiffel Tower

WE TURNED A CORNER by a tall granite building, and there it was the goal of our short, sightseeing tour of Paris—the Eiffel Tower.

My daughter, Marnie, and I had met at the Charles de Gaulle Aero port early on the morning of July 26, 2001. We had met because her earthly mother and her Heavenly Father persuaded me that she shouldn't travel home alone from Africa, or be alone in Paris for a ten-hour layover. With our connections working out perfectly, we figured we had at least six hours to see some of the sights in "the city of lights" before we headed home to Maine. Top on our list was the Eiffel Tower and Notre Dame Cathedral. We had traveled the B Line into the city from the airport, and then we took a city bus to the C Line from Saint Michel's. The rest of the trip to the tower was on foot as we mingled with the tourists and citizens of the city on the crowded two blocks to one of the seven wonders of the modern world.

As we strolled, hand-in-hand, to the base of the "grand erector set," Marnie's eye quickly left the towering tower and wandered to a street vendor just in front of the entrance to the park. She had left Africa late in the afternoon of the day before. After forty-four days of village food, she was ready for some real food, and her first craving was ice cream—rich,

French vanilla ice cream! I quickly got out twenty francs and paid the vendor for an extra-big scoop. Marnie attacked that ice cream cone as if it was her first meal in six weeks, and maybe, if the truth were told, it was. With each lick, the smile on her face grew larger. As we walked under the Eiffel Tower, she licked and looked, but I was watching her carefully. It reminded me of her reaction when she was four and I would do something special for her. I will never, ever forget that ice cream under the world's most famous tower, or the smile it brought to my daughter's face, or the sheer joy that came to my heart.

As we roamed beneath the mammoth monument, Marnie slowly ate her Paris ice cream cone. It was a warm, bright day, so she had to lick quickly! As we explored for the perfect angle to take our picture together (her mother and my wife had made me promise I would get a picture of us near the Eiffel Tower as a remembrance of our time in Paris), the ice cream cone slowly disappeared until the last bit had been consumed. Our quest for the camera shot continued, but I thought, "If so be ye have tasted that the Lord is gracious" (1 Peter 2:3). Wouldn't it be great if people would get as much pleasure out of Christ as my daughter got out of her Paris ice cream cone?

When was the last time you enjoyed a piece of the Word of God with such passion? When was the last time your time of prayer was as memorable as an ice cream cone under the Eiffel Tower? Does your time spent with Christ bring you such simple pleasure as I witnessed that day with Marnie?

Only you can answer these questions and explain your answers!

## 25

## Downtown Park

I AM A HISTORIAN by my very nature, and when I realized I would be spending a morning and afternoon in downtown Paris, I began to rehearse in my mind what I remembered best about Paris from the history books I had read. I knew from the start that I would only be able to get a brief glimpse of the mighty metropolis, but I was going to at least see as much as I could and recall even more.

My daughter and I arrived by subway into the very heart of the city about mid-morning. Because part of the subway was under construction, we had come up at Saint Michel's just down the street from Notre Dame Cathedral (we could see it from where we caught the city bus to the Eiffel Tower). We followed the Seine River on its south side, passing the Muse due Louvre, which was on the north side of the river. The bus continued along the river for a few miles before turning onto the Boulevard de la Tour Maubourg. It wasn't until later that I checked my map and discovered that we were just across from the famous Avenue des Champs Elysees. We were three days too early to see Lance Armstrong peddle his way down that avenue to win his third Tour de France. Of course, at the head of that world famous street is the Arche Triomphe. This landmark was on my "to see" list because of my love of Napoleonic history, but I never saw it.

Marnie and I reentered the subway at a place called Invalides; I don't know why it was called that, but eventually we came back to the surface at Quai Branly. We walked the sidewalks through vendors and tourists and artists until we were standing together beneath the Eiffel Tower. It was impressive, but as for me, the Parc du Champ de Mars was even more impressive. This huge park, like the Mall in Washington, DC (minus the reflection pool), is a grand garden with beautiful flowers and wonderful shade tree paths. The lawn was green and lush, and the atmosphere was like Grand Central Park in New York: a bit of country in a busy city. It might seem strange with all the costly edifies we passed to get to the shadow of the tower, but this I know, I liked the park best.

It was early afternoon by the time Marnie and I had our picture taken in the middle of that park with the tower in the background. A couple from Australia, interestingly, did the honor for us, as we in turn took their picture. Our time in downtown Paris was slipping away quickly, but instead of moving on to other historical sites, Marnie and I chose to wander hand-in-hand around the Parc du Champ de Mars. It just reminded me that in all of human history, civilization began in a park, not a city (Genesis 2:8). And for as long as man has built his cities, he always seems to need to put a park in the middle of it. Why? Could it be that he knows that his first conversation with God was in a garden, not a gutter? It is refreshing to know that not matter how far this "country boy" roams, he can always find a park, even if it is in downtown Paris!

## 26

## The Eiffel Tower

WHAT IS IT ABOUT mankind and towers?

As I stand under the most famous tower still standing in the world, I cannot help but remember the first tower ever constructed by man:

> And they said, Go to, let us build a city and a tower, whose top may reach unto heaven; and let us make us a name, lest we be scattered abroad upon the face of the whole earth. (Genesis 11:4)

The more history changes, the less history changes! The first tower project was started, if not finished, under the direction of a man named Nimrod (Genesis 10:8–10). His tower became world-famous, but instead of bearing his name, it was named by God Himself, and He called it Babel (Genesis 11:9).

As I gazed with my daughter up into the mid-day sun, it also appeared to us that the Eiffel Tower reached the sky. It is an amazing structure, and as we walked under its mammoth mass, I recalled its history. Alexandre Gustave Eiffel was the mastermind behind this tower. Best known for the tower that bares his name, we Americans should not forget that it is Eiffel's steel framework that keeps the Statue of Liberty standing tall in New York Harbor. Eiffel was born in Dijon, France, in 1832, and by twenty-nine he was building railroad bridges out of iron. He would eventually build these bridges in Europe, Africa, and Asia. He was one of the first to realize that iron construction took half as long to build, at half the cost of building with stone.

Eiffel's famous tower was built for the 1889 World's Fair in Paris. At the time of its construction, it was the tallest man-made structure in the world (985 feet), something else it has in common with the Tower of Babel. The tower cost a million dollars, but the French government had only promised Eiffel a quarter of that. Most thought the tower that reached the clouds would bankrupt Eiffel, but once he charged admission to climb the tower, he earned back almost all the expense in the first year. He earned nothing from Marnie and me, for we both preferred to walk the park and look at the tower rather than climb it. Many, however, were still paying after one-hundred-and-twelve years to climb Eiffel's tower to see the sights from the top.

As I watched the busloads of tourists pull up to the tower and stand in line to make the hike up its height, I thought of what it must have been like at Babel. Were there tours as well? The one sad truth that came to me was that like Babel, these people were not climbing the tower to get a better view of God, but of the city. If only the people of Babylon would have used their tower to get to know God better, I think that city and tower would still be standing today. But mankind hasn't changed! A city with a tower has been built in just about every country in the world. This is not unique with France, but what is consistent about these great cities and their towers is that they are constructed so people can look down and around, but not above (Colossians 3:2)!

## 27

## Unimpressed with Paris

From the train rolling into Paris, I look out its windows into the little villages that line the tracks before the great metropolis comes into view. My daughter, Marnie, and I are taking half a morning and half an afternoon to see as much of "the city" as we can before heading back to the States.

When I flew into Charles de Gaulle Aero port this morning, my first thought was that the pilot had taken me west instead of east. France looked like Kansas, and the flat fields and small towns were in full summer attire. A checkerboard of crops and colors were all I could see, and there certainly wasn't any big city in sight. I was expecting rolling hills and many people, and all I saw was land as level as the American plains. Now as I ride the rails into Paris, I see no huge factories or high rises. All the train window reveals are tiny rustic hamlets with plenty of trash lying everywhere. I expected neat and clean, and all I see is garbage and graffiti, and what I saw in the countryside, I see in the city. The most beautiful city in the world wasn't very beautiful after all!

Because of construction on the tracks, Marnie and I couldn't take the train all the way to the Eiffel Tower. Our first stop brought us up into the very heart of the city. As we waited for the city bus by the Seine River, I saw trash on the sidewalks and under the bridges. Despite the fact there were trashcans on every corner, nobody seemed to use them. People were throwing things everywhere. Dirty streets, disgusting alleyways and unhelpful people were my first impressions of Paris. Granted, neither Marnie nor I could speak French, (even though I took two years in high school, my French teacher would have been so ashamed of me) and perhaps, the Parisians didn't want to bother, for the directions they gave us to help us got us lost! How hard is it to find the most famous tower in the world? Marnie and I wasted a lot of our time in Paris wandering the unkempt streets, trying to find our way through the maze.

Oh, the buildings were impressive, as each was old and ornate. I must admit I have never much cared for statues: the idols of the past. One man's art and another man's culture have never impressed me either. You would have heard no 'oohs' or 'ahhs' escaping my lips as I wandered with my daughter, up and down the streets around the Eiffel Tower. Marnie and I were searching for some French tea for my wife, but all we found were more dirty streets and unhelpful people. I saw in Paris what Paul saw in Athens:

> Now while Paul waited for them at Athens, his spirit was stirred in him, when he saw the city wholly given to idolatry. (Acts 17:16)

Paris seems to be a city totally ignorant of the True and Living God!

I know I am just a "hayseed" from Maine, and most will never read of my impressions of Paris. I am a "yokel" and a "Yankee," and I will probably never, ever again visit the city by the Seine, but for what it is worth: save your money and come visit me in Maine, and I'll show you some God-made wilderness that will put Paris' man-made wonders to shame!

## 28

## Detour

According to Vance Havner, I have arrived at spiritual maturity, for he says:

> It has been said that a mark of deep spiritual maturity is to be able to enjoy the journey when God puts you on a detour!

Marnie and I had finished a six-hour side trip to the Eiffel Tower and were heading back to the airport when we got lost. We had retraced our bus ride and train ride into the city when we stopped at Anlnay Sous-Bois to let some passengers off. As the train door closed, Marnie said, "Bubby, I hope we weren't supposed to get off here." Her traveling instinct was right, for within a few miles we saw a sign that read "Sevran Livry": God had taken us on a detour.

Life itself has detours. An old preacher once said:

> We set out upon the highway of some fixed course we have chosen and mapped and planned for ourselves. Then one day around some sudden bend of the road, we find our thoroughfare blocked and a side road in its place. Business crashes, health fails, dear ones die, disaster comes; we must abandon the way we meant to go and try some shabby trail of shattered dreams and fallen hopes and breaking hearts. We start out wearily upon it and find to our

surprise that it leads to treasures and beauty we never would have found elsewhere!

When John Bunyan was detoured through Bedford Prison, he wrote *Pilgrim's Progress*. When Paul ran into the Damascus detour (Acts 9:3), he was led down glorious roads of service he never would have traveled if not for that detour. And so it will be with us.

At 19, I was traveling down an easy road, but I was asleep at the spiritual wheel. I was speeding down the road of my life with no direction or destination, but the scenery was pleasant and the road smooth. It was then I came upon my detour, and I was sent in an entirely different direction. At first, I was unsure of its virtue over the main road I was traveling, but the farther I follow this narrow road, the more I am sure it is the better road. Unlike the road I was on, this detour can't be traveled quickly. I am forced to stop and look around and see the world around me, as I have on this trip to Paris. On the super highway of self-will, the scenery was nothing but a blur. Now the road is clear, and the way is lined with wonderful blessings I would have missed if I hadn't taken God's detour!

We must believe that despite the detour, God's side roads in life do hold their own compensations. Whether a crushing detour that takes you from a rosy road to a drab driveway of infirmity, or a running path of success to plodding along a difficult lane with one misfortune after another; when the journey is over and we look back on this burdensome boulevard, we will conclude with Paul, "I have finished my course" (2 Timothy 4:7), detours and all!

Our detour in Paris was only about 30 minutes in length, but as with others in my past, I enjoyed the company the best!

✈

## 29

## Pooped Out in Paris

By the time I met Marnie in France, I had been on the road or in the air for nearly twenty hours. I do believe I did have a short, thirty-minute nap on the plane just as I neared Paris, but that was it. Nevertheless, when the plane landed, my second wind kicked in and I was ready for a quick trip into downtown Paris with my daughter.

It took us an hour or so to work through the crowds and customs on our way to the RER—the local rail system. It took us another forty minutes of walking, riding, and busing to get to the Eiffel Tower, our primary sightseeing destination. Despite all the modern modes of transport, I was surprised just how much walking Marnie and I had to do between terminals, bus stops and subway tunnels. Marnie had huge blisters on her heels by the time we made it to the Tower. Oh, I forgot to tell you about all the walking we had to do to find a place to exchange my dollars into francs. (The moneychangers in the Temple of Jerusalem were alive and well at the Charles de Gaulle Aero port!) Then we wandered the back streets around the Tower in search of a gift for my wife. We were looking for some French tea, but French people don't seem to drink much tea!

By the time Marnie and I got back to Terminal #1 around mid-afternoon, I had been up and on the move for twenty-six hours, and Marnie for longer than that. (We also did some extra walking when Marnie and I got on the wrong train, heading to Sevran Livry instead of the airport! We walked around the village of Sevran Livry until we found our mistake and figured out how to correct it!) My fifty-year-old body was beginning to rebel, but before I could even think about relaxing and resting on the seven-and-a-half hour flight back to Boston, Marnie and I still had to clear our tickets and find Coleen some tea. So we walked some more. Because the ticket counter was so poorly marked, we passed it by and walked the length of the terminal only to discover our counter was where we had started. Once we finally located our gate (more walking), all I wanted to do was find a seat, but only after walking through all the little shops in the terminal to get rid of my final francs. Marnie and I were finally able after much searching to locate some French tea and a cup and saucer for my dear wife.

I was into my twenty-eighth hour when I turned to my daughter and announced, "I'm pooped out in Paris!" She smiled and said, "Amen!" I tried to remember if I had ever experienced such a sleepless stretch in my life—I hadn't! Despite the tired legs and tender feet, my spirits were still very strong because by God's grace I had accomplished my quest. It reminded me of these words from the pen of Paul:

> For which cause we faint not; but though our outward man perish, yet the inward man is renewed day by day. (2 Corinthians 4:16)

It is wonderful to know that even when we are pooping out in Paris, God is pouring into us His special strength, so we can finish our day and complete our task.

## 30

## Old Cathedrals

For these, my last few hours in France, I must forego a nap and another shopping spree to write an observation that is positive about my time in downtown Paris. I know I have shared already many negative opinions about my first trip to the city by the Seine, but ponder this if you will!

One of our last journeys in Paris was a slow bus ride by Notre Dame Cathedral. We didn't have time to stop because of our late afternoon flight and our desire to walk the park around the Eiffel Tower. As we made our way past the famous chapel through heavy "heading home" traffic toward Saint Michel's bus stop, I snapped a few pictures of the grandest cathedral of them all. Time didn't allow us to stop and go inside, but it wasn't what was inside that I was most inspired by. As I viewed the amazing architecture and artistry, I was reminded of this devotional by Henry Bosch from the "Our Daily Bread" staff. I have been a fan of this devotional booklet since I was a child. I still use their wonderfully written articles for illustrations in my sermons. What I remembered and recalled as I viewed Notre Dame was this:

> Many of the old cathedrals in France are very beautiful on the inside, but their exteriors are adorned with figures depicting animals with hideously distorted features. Inquiring about this strange fact,

a traveler was told that the builders in the Middle Ages wanted these images to represent man's sinful appetites and prejudices. They were therefore placed on the outside of the buildings as a reminder to worshipers that if they expected to sense the presence of God, then they should leave bitterness, wrath and selfish attitudes outside the sanctuary. To approach Him, they were to come with pure hearts. Whether or not this was actually in the mind of the medieval architects we don't know, but the concept does emphasize an important truth about worshiping in the house of God . . . the apostle Paul speaks to a company of believers in 1 Corinthians 11 who were coming together for worship and the Lord's Supper in a careless manner. One of their number was engaged in immorality (1 Corinthians 5:1), and the members were viewing this with a haughty attitude. So Paul had to remind them to keep the feast not with malice and wickedness, but with sincerity and truth (1 Corinthians 5:8). We must prepare ourselves for worship by leaving any sinful attitudes outside the church. If we harbor animosity towards others, we should ask God to remove it. In this way, we will maintain the unity of the Spirit and help to ensure that Sunday will be a blessed day in the house of the Lord.

If you want to be spiritually fed on Sunday, go to church with a good appetite, not a bad attitude! I saw this concept clearly as I viewed Notre Dame Cathedral from the window of a slow moving city bus; one of the positive lessons I learned from my short time in Paris. And it is my hope and desire that one of the reasons I was taken to Paris was to pass on these spiritual insights to those who have gotten caught up in the exterior of their faith to the neglect of the interior of their heart!

## 31

## Speaking One to Another

I HAD TRAVELED THOUSANDS of miles with hundreds of people, but it wasn't until I met my daughter in Paris that I found someone who spoke my language. I am not writing of the English language, but of Christian conversation.

Few, even among believers, speak one to the other of the things of the Lord. My daughter, Marnie, is one of those rare exceptions. Almost from the day she could talk, she spoke of the ways of God. She developed early a love of talking about the Lord, despite the fact that 'Christian' isn't spoken much anymore. God has always had a desire that:

> They that feared the Lord speak often one to another: and the Lord hearkened, and heard it, and a book of remembrance was written before him for them that feared the Lord, and that thought upon his name. (Malachi 3:16)

Is this one of the reasons I came to Paris, so that another chapter of that "book of remembrance" could be written?

Almost from our first words at the Charles de Gaulle Aeroport, Marnie and I have been relating to each other how our God has spoken to us over the last few weeks. Despite the fact that we had been separated by an ocean, that "still, small voice" was loud and clear. We both had things to learn as our Heavenly Father directed our summers. Little did we know when we were separated in June that in July we would be sharing the road to Paris! And so it has been down through Church history. Christ has always had His few praising His name. From the famous family of Noah and the days of the flood when only eight spoke the language (1 Peter 3:20) to the days of Elijah when only 7,000 were fluent in the tongue of the King (1 Kings 19:18). Whether the Christians in Rome during the days of the catacomb conversations, or the days in Germany during the Reformation, Christ has always had His twos and threes speaking one to the other of His glorious grace and marvelous mercy!

Marnie and I found it easy in the midst of the crowd to speak freely of how the Lord had brought us together in France. Those we could understand were talking about the American, Lance Armstrong, and how he was going to win his third Tour de France bicycle race and of his triumphal ride into Paris on Sunday, but little did they know of the two Christians that rode triumphantly into Paris on Thursday morning (2 Corinthians 2:14). They were unnoticed by the throng, and there was no cheering from the masses, but my daughter and I had just finished a forty-four-day marathon that will, in my opinion, survive anything those bicyclists have accomplished. They rode for an earthly reward, my daughter and I for a heavenly one.

Why is this? It is because our citizenship is in Heaven (Ephesians 2:19) and our "mother tongue" is the language of the Almighty. So as we prepare to leave the French and their strange tongue, we are also prepared to leave this world for another world where everyone speaks the same language.

## 32

## Open Window

THIS MUST SEEM A strange title for a devotional on a trip to Paris by air-conditioned buses, through air-conditioned terminals, and on air-conditioned planes. The open window is not a part of modern travel, and according to this pattern, I didn't sit next to an open window until my daughter and I hopped a subway train that took us into the city of Paris. I am thinking of our 'open window' experiences in the French capitol as we set behind closed windows again awaiting our flight out of France.

I can honestly say with the disciples, when the Lord asked them:

> When I sent you without purse, and scrip, and shoes, lacked ye any thing? And they said, "Nothing!" (Luke 22:35)

I too have lacked nothing on this unexpected odyssey to rendezvous with my daughter in Paris. I would rather be an individual fully trusting in the Lord that will lack nothing than a man who has everything and lacks God. I have become convinced on this journey that we will lack nothing when we travel at His bidding, whether to the next city or the next continent! It was said of the early saints, "Neither was there any among them that lacked . . ." (Acts 4:34).

It was true then and it is true now because of this marvelous promise: "But my God shall supply all your need according to his riches in glory by Christ Jesus" (Philippians 4:19). In the world the windows are closed, but in Christ I travel with an open window. "Prove me now herewith, saith the Lord of hosts, if I will not open you the windows of heaven, and pour you out a blessing, that there shall not be room enough to receive it" (Malachi 3:10).

The world is like the cynical question of 2 Kings 7:2:

> Then a lord on whose hand the king leaned answered the man of God and said, "Behold, if the Lord would make windows in heaven, might this thing be?"

So the world seals its windows and tries to provide for itself, little realizing that God will weigh out for them far beyond what they could produce for themselves. The pen of Paul puts it this way, "But as it is written, 'Eye hath not seen, nor ear heard, neither have entered into the heart of man, the things which God hath prepared for them that love him'" (2 Corinthians 2:9). God doesn't want us to live in a sealed room; He has not doomed us to a desert existence; He has opened His heavenly windows, and He wants to pour us out such a blessing that we can't hold or handle it all. This is how my daughter and I felt as we talked together in the Charles de Gaulle Aero port outside Paris, France.

I like what Vance Havner has written about this concept of God's blessings:

> The man who walks with God can afford to let the man of this world take his choice. The meek shall inherit the earth and the saints shall judge it. So everything will be ours eventually anyway. What the

millionaires of this age do not know is that they are only renters!

Vance's millionaires are billionaires today, but this truth is still the same!

# 33

## Heading Home

Today I watched the milling crowd from under the shadow of the Eiffel Tower; they looked lost and lonely. I like what Vance Havner once said about loneliness: "We've never had more amusement and entertainment than we have today, but we've never had more lonely people." I saw this in the "city of lights" and wondered why?

From a terminal at the Charles de Gaulle Aero port, I am watching people read the paper, trying to make sense of an insane world. Others are strolling along in deep thought by my daughter and me, but I wonder if their thoughts are on God? Still others are hurrying by as if they are going somewhere, but I wonder if their somewhere will lead them anywhere. Despite the confusion and commotion, Marnie and I are not bewildered or bothered because we are heading home. I only left home a little over twenty-five hours ago, while Marnie has been away for forty-four days. Yet we are heading home together, and there is nothing quite like the feeling of homeward bound!

Forgive me for spiritualizing just a bit, but isn't that the problem with mankind today? They are away from home, alone and lonely! Our real home is with God! Sin has led us away from home, just like the prodigal in Jesus' famous story (Luke 15). And like our forefather, Cain, we have been a fugitive and vagabond wandering far away from home. I met a man on my flight to Paris that has no place on earth to call home. The son of a Canadian diplomat in Germany, he traveled during all of his childhood and has continued that wandering into his adulthood. I could tell by his voice that he envied me just a bit, and not because I was going to Paris! No, it was because I was going home by way of Paris, and not alone. Marnie and I have reached the zenith of our trip, and despite the fact that we still have nearly fourteen hours left, we both know we are heading in the right direction, and not by ourselves.

So it is when the sinner meets his Savior. He has made the last corner, managed the final curve, and turned into the "narrow way" (Matthew 7:14) that leads home. Dear saint, don't let the world convince you that thinking of "home" is strange or odd. Paul wrote:

> For me to live is Christ, and to die is gain. But if I live in the flesh, this is the fruit of my labor; yet what shall I choose I wot not. For I am in a strait betwixt two, having a desire to depart, and to be with Christ; which is far better: nevertheless to abide in the flesh is more needful for you. (Philippians 1:21–24)

Like Marnie and I in Paris, we are just pilgrims and strangers, tourists in an alien town, and we both just want to go home. We are weary. We are tired. We even had a chance to stay an extra day because the airline had overbooked our flight out of France. I'll never forget what my daughter said to the ticket agent when she was asked to stay: "I have been traveling for forty-four days, and I want to go home!" We as Christians ought to feel that same thrill about our expected departure, a journey that will take us home to heaven!

# 34

## 24 Hours

According to the speed indicator, Marnie and I are winging our way home at 588 miles per hour. We are cruising at 32,000 feet high over the Atlantic Ocean. At last count, we had flown 1,731 miles from Paris, but still had 1,827 miles to go before we arrive in Boston. If we are on time, I will have made a trip from America to France and back within twenty-four hours. It is amazing to me what the Good Lord can accomplish in a day when He wants to. "Lead me in thy truth, and teach me: for thou art the God of my salvation; on thee do I wait all day" (Psalms 25:5).

I left America from Philadelphia at 7 p.m. last night. If the headwind isn't too bad, Marnie and I will land in our homeland around 6 p.m. tonight with an hour to spare. According to the plane's mile-o-meter, that will be a round trip of over 7,000 miles. And when you consider that I spent from 7:15 a.m. to 4:30 p.m. touring Paris, that will be quite an accomplishment for a farmer's son that now has been overseas only twice in his fifty years. This laid-back country preacher isn't used to covering that distance in a day.

Besides the flight time, I traveled by train and bus from the Charles de Gaulle Aero port to the Eiffel Tower and Notre Dame Cathedral. It was a whirlwind ride, or maybe a race to see how much my daughter and I could see of Paris during our layover. It was amazing to me that neither of us had ever traveled into Paris, yet the miles we covered in uncharted territory were also accomplished within the twenty-four-hour span. As I continue my trip back across the Atlantic Ocean, I am more convinced than ever that if God could get me through such a day, then He can do anything in a day:

> Day One: He could create the light and divide the light from the darkness and name them Day and Night. (Genesis 1:3–5)
>
> Day Two: He could create a firmament by dividing the waters from the waters and naming it Heaven. (Genesis 1:6–8)
>
> Day Three: He could gather the waters together and let the dry land appear and name them Sea and Earth. (Genesis 1:9–13)
>
> Day Four: He could create a great light and a lesser light in the heavens and make "the stars also." (Genesis 1:14–19)
>
> Day Five: He could create fowl for the air and fish for the sea and cause them to multiply. (Genesis 1:20–23)
>
> Day Six: He could create creatures to inhabit the land, including man: the crown of His creation. (Genesis 1:24–31)

My twenty-four hours back and forth across the Atlantic Ocean was just a reminder to me and to the evolutionists of what God can do in a day, any day, when He sets His mind to it!

# 35

## "The Kid"

MARNIE AND I JUST finished watching a funny flick called "The Kid" with Bruce Willis and the funniest child actor I have ever seen. It has allowed us a few minutes to unwind from a very busy day and a half while winging our way farther west: closer and closer to our final destination—home!

If you have never seen the movie, it is about a guy who gets a chance to relive his childhood when he was eight years old. The kid in him had something to teach the almost forty-year-old adult. It reminded me of what has happened in my life over the last 33 hours. I too have been able to laugh again because of the young person sitting next to me. For the last 14 hours, my 21-year-old daughter has made me feel like a kid again.

We have laughed and lived the life of two carefree tourists walking and wandering our way through Paris. If she hadn't been with me, I would never in a million years have ventured alone into that downtown dungeon. I wouldn't have even come on this trip if it weren't for her. As I ponder this concept, I recall these words of Paul:

> When I was a child, I spake as a child, I understood as a child, I thought as a child; but when I became a man, I put away childish things. For now we see

> through a glass, darkly; but then face to face: now
> I know in part; but then shall I know even as also I
> am known. (1 Corinthians 13:11–12)

I am fifty-something, not forty, and Marnie is twenty-one, not eight, but I have just lived the story of "The Kid." Marnie has taught me on this trip to "go for it," to expand my borders and explore my world, and be a kid again, if only for a few hours. We adults get too much into our routines and routes that we forget to be carefree. To be fancy-free once in a while isn't a bad thing, and to wander the streets of Paris with a beautiful twenty-one-year-old on your arm is quite thrilling! To feel the freedom of no worries, if only for a few hours, was worth the trip. It seemed the more I escaped America, the more I escaped my old life. I can see now that the kid in Paris wasn't my daughter; it was me!

Once again I take a look at our trip map across the Atlanta Ocean, and it says we have flown 3,000 miles with only 552 to go until we reach Boston. It has been a marvelous adventure and an eye-opening experience. I have learned that to put away "childish things" doesn't mean you can't be a kid again. The "kid" in Paris is about ready to reenter his world, but like Bruce Willis' character, I will return a different man, for the boy in Barry had a chance to stretch his legs again, even if for just a few short hours in Paris. I come back with new insights into the workings of a twenty-one-year-old and why I have nothing to fear in turning over the Lord's work to young people like her. The Church will survive just fine because the Good Lord is called those who are not confined to borders and boundaries like their Dads!

## 36

## Winging on West

This will be my last observation on our trip back across the Atlantic Ocean. I have, however, jotted down a few more topics to be explored when I finally get back home. No doubt after I rest, I will be able to add a few more insights to this mission to Paris. My mind is getting a bit fuzzy since I have been on the road for nearly a day and a half.

We are at present nearing the end to an interesting Trans-Atlantic crossing. Unlike my flight going over, which was pretty much a direct route from Philadelphia to Paris; we have taken the northern path this time. According to the flight map, we left Paris and flew first to the southern tip of England, then over Ireland and then toward Greenland. The pilot has just announced that we are passing Goose Bay, Labrador. In our winging westward, we have actually flown north and are now heading south to Boston. Our journey will actually take us over our home state of Maine. It is interesting that we will fly over Bangor, our final destination, on our way to Logan International Airport.

As I write these final few lines, Marnie has closed her eyes for a minute. According to her, I caught a few winks myself at the tail end of the onboard movie. She is tired after forty-four days away from home and all the physical problems she developed in Togo. All I can say is, "Thanks for the ride!" Thanks to my Traveling Companion for the safe flights. "Praise Him for His mighty acts; praise Him according to His excellent greatness" (Psalms 150:2). Thanks to my daughter for allowing me to be a part of her great adventure, and thanks to all those who made this rendezvous in Paris possible. Thanks and many more thanks!

As we wing our way west, albeit southwest, I stop for a final time to say to my dear Guide, "It was a perfect journey!" I say to my Companion, "The Company was pleasant and the trip insightful." I say to my Travel Agent, "I couldn't have done it without your amazing scheduling." I say to my Pilot, "The flights were all smooth and on time." I wish I could live the rest of my life with the same level of peace, confidence and direction I had on this trip to Europe and back. I have sensed the Lord's presence every step of the way, and I have heard His voice as clear as I have ever heard it. I have discovered that He can speak on a plane, a train, a bus, or just walking the streets of Paris; strolling under a famous tower, or at 32,000 feet; that still, small voice is still precious.

I go back to Maine, back to the ministry, a different man, father, husband and pastor. My prayer is that when I take up my responsibilities again, I will not soon lose the lessons that I learned on this expedition to Europe. That I will always realize that whether Europe or Ellsworth, I still travel with the same Companion, directed by the same Guide, scheduled by the same Agent, and piloted by the same Pilot! May I always be thankful for such a God?

## 37

## Blessed Downcastings

I'VE HEARD IT SAID numerous times before I left for Paris, "Isn't it too bad Marnie got sick in Africa?" But I didn't meet a discouraged disciple in France. Instead, I met a young missionary rejoicing over the blessings she discovered in her sickness. I think we all have much to learn from "blessed downcastings" (A Charles Spurgeon term).

Does this devotional find you in the grip of "fiery trials?"

> Beloved, think it not strange concerning the fiery trials which is to try you, as though some strange thing happened unto you. (1 Peter 4:12)

Are you embattled with foes before, behind, beside and even beneath? Others speak of wonderful summers, while you come down with worms! Others sail through calm seas, while you fight a raging sea of doubt and dread! You don't go so far as to blame God, but you are wondering, why me? A young Christian from Maine faced such trials in a strange land amongst a strange people who spoke a strange language, but she, like Peter, thought it not strange! How strange?

My dear daughter has learned this summer the "lesson of lingering" in the hands of the Almighty—that delicate place where it is only the hands of the Lord that are holding you up. Far away from family and friends, she only had Him to trust. All the great ones in Christianity have learned to abandon all to Jesus. David wrote of it in the Psalms when he was fleeing King Saul alone. Augustine wrote of it in his famous "Confession." Read of the life of John Bunyan and he speaks of it as well, and what of David Brainard, alone in a horrible land with hostile savages finding this wonderful blessing Spurgeon called "blessed downcastings."

If you've had a good look into the depths of your heart in a time of deep trial and found Him, then you have been and are blessed. My heart swelled and my tears fell as I heard Marnie tell of this lesson learned in the testing of Togo. I put a young lady on a plane in early June heading for Africa, and by the end of July I was flying home with a seasoned saint to Maine. As the mission doctors and nurses were treating Marnie's symptoms, God was treating her soul. The Great Physician was getting at the real disease of her life—the disease of wonder and worry.

My daughter returned with me from Paris weak physically, but strong spiritually. She had learned to "abide in me, and I in you. As the branch cannot bear fruit of itself, except it abide in the vine; no more can ye, except ye abide in me" (John 15:4). Though Marnie had never read him, I believe she discerned as the great preacher Spurgeon once described:

Blessed downcasts that drive us to Thee, O Lord!

If you would ask my daughter today, she would say her greatest lessons in Africa were learned in sickness and sorrow, not in service and supplication.

# 38

## Borrow Tomorrow?

> Take therefore no thought for tomorrow: for the morrow shall take thought for the things of itself. Sufficient unto the day is the evil thereof. (Matthew 6:34)

ON MY QUICK TRIP to Paris to rendezvous with my daughter, I carried this "time table" in my pocket:

| EVENTS | PLANNED TIMES | ACTUAL |
|---|---|---|
| Leave Ellsworth | 7:00 a.m. | 6:50 a.m. |
| Leave Bangor | 8:15 a.m. | 8:20 a.m. |
| Leave Portland | 10:30 a.m. | 10:40 a.m. |
| Leave South Station | 12:25 p.m. | 12:35 p.m. |
| Arrive Logan Airport | 12:45 p.m. | 12:55 p.m. |
| Leave Boston | 2:45 p.m. | 2:05 p.m. |
| Arrive Philadelphia | 4:14 p.m. | 3:05 p.m. |
| Leave Philadelphia | 6:05 p.m. | 7:05 p.m. |
| Arrive Paris | 1:40 a.m. | 1:33 a.m. |
| Leave Paris | 9:55 a.m. | 10:30 a.m. |
| Arrive Boston | 5:45 p.m. | 5:35 p.m. |
| Leave Boston | 8:00 p.m. | 9:21 p.m. |
| Arrive Bangor | 9:25 p.m. | 10:00 p.m. |
| Arrive Ellsworth | 11:00 p.m. | 11:15 p.m. |

(All times are on "Maine Time.")

I learned a valuable lesson on my trip to Paris and back. Notice how closely my planned schedule and the actual schedule were! There is no need to "borrow tomorrow" when you have the Lord on your side. This was reinforced when I got back to Maine and read this devotional by Dennis DeHaan:

> Do you want to overcome worry? Then accept each day as a new and precious gift from God. Live it to the fullest. Learn to be a good steward of time. Discipline yourself to plan for your future, but don't live in it. When Pastor Ed Dobson learned that his friend Ed Keats from Danville, Virginia, had cancer, he immediately went to see him. Keats said, "I just found out I have cancer. The doctor broke the news as gently as possible and told me I had but two days to live. I said to him, 'That's the best news I've had in a long time.' Startled, the doctor asked, 'What do you mean?' Keats replied, 'Over the years I've learned to trust God for just one day at a time, and now you are giving me two days? I'd call that good news.'"

Sure, God changes our plans a bit, but as you can see from the timetable above, only a bit. I challenge you to take some forty hours of your life and do as I did, and I believe you too will discover that what is planned will happen within minutes. If this is true, then why do we 'borrow tomorrow?'

# 39

## Sufficient

I NEVER KNEW THE real, spiritual meaning of the word "sufficient" until I made an unexpected trip to Paris, France, to rendezvous with my daughter on her homeward journey from Togo, West Africa. What a grand Biblical word!

Because every day has its own share of difficulties, what is the value of borrowing from tomorrow? Is there any profit from getting to Paris before you get to Portland? If I learned anything on my trip to Europe, it was to let the moments of each hour simply come as they came and not worry if I would be late for my flight to Paris while I was still waiting for my flight to Philadelphia. In each aspect of my odyssey I found the Lord to be "sufficient," for He cleared up whatever troubles there might have been.

Most people like me need a dramatic demonstration of God's amazing "sufficiency" to help us quit worrying and fretting over the twists and turns of our lives. For me, it has been this trip to Paris. I have been jolted into the reality that my God is bigger than Maine, and that He is in control of events in America and Africa. I serve a worldwide Savior, and I need not fuss or fume, because God is here and there. I found that out of my comfort zone, His provision was sufficient, as was His person. I heard with Paul:

> My grace is sufficient for thee. (2 Corinthians 12:9)

He can supply sufficient patience when you're waiting a delayed flight to Paris. He can supply sufficient rest to run a 7,000-plus mile marathon in forty hours. He can supply sufficient grace to work your way through the maze that is Paris and to spend a few blissful moments with your daughter on the Parc de Camp du Mars. He can supply sufficient perseverance to wade through the numerous ticket counters at the Charles de Gaulle Aero port to finally find the gate that will lead you back home. He can supply sufficient funds to pull this once-in-a-lifetime adventure off, and He can supply sufficient helpers along the way to make it a pleasant task versus a miserable job. He can supply sufficient prayer warriors to pray for you through each step of the journey from Ellsworth to Europe and back again. And He did!

I know God doesn't have favorites: "I perceive that God is no respecter of persons" (Acts 10:34), but on this trip abroad I felt special enough to believe just the opposite because of the sufficiency He showed me and my daughter. If I didn't know better, it seemed like He was moving the entire world so that I could get to Paris to meet my daughter at the end of that very, very long ramp. Then he moved Paris around so that we could relax and unwind from the emotion and excitement of our different trips. He moved again to get us safely home. Here before me is one of the reasons I traveled all day and all night and all day again: to discover the "sufficiency" of my Savior in sudden situations, for "sufficient unto the DAY is the evil thereof" (Matthew 6:34), and could I add the "goodness" thereof as well, for He is "sufficient" in both!

## 40

## Eloquent Etiquette

I HAD BEEN LISTENING to the television talk shows and the radio reports about the mess the air transportation industry is in. I had heard about the delays and cancellations and layovers. Since I have just returned from a flight to Paris, I feel I can now speak with some authority on the subject.

As I got on the bus for Boston, I expected to face a mess on my path to Paris to rendezvous with my daughter. But I found no messes in the buses or planes. My travels from Bangor to Boston, Philadelphia to Paris, were carefree and comfortable. I found that even when I was delayed, I still got to my destination on time. I discovered that most travel lines have built in delays already in their schedules. For example, I left Philly one hour behind schedule, but I still made it to the Charles de Gaulle Aero port on time! On our return flight from France, Marnie and I left Paris late, yet we still managed to make it to Boston on schedule. And as for the people in the transportation industry, I never met a flight attendant, bus driver, ticket agent, or local janitor that wasn't polite, kind and helpful, as were all my fellow passengers!

I had left home with "air rage" stories in my brain and terminal shootings on my mind, yet I saw nothing coming close to either. I sat beside a Canadian whose TV didn't work for the six-and-a-half hour flight from Philly to Paris, yet I never heard a swear word from his lips, nor did he get mad at the flight attendants. Despite the number of times he asked for help and found nobody that could get the television working, he remained calm and cheerful. On the other side of me was a young French girl heading home who had to go straight to work when she arrived in Paris! She found it hard to sleep, but she was nothing short of pleasant and sweet. I left home with my extra money hidden, thinking everybody was a pickpocket, yet I found nobody a threat or a thief. I never once felt threatened or that somebody was after what I had. I never felt afraid or scared, whether on the bus or in the air. I walked mile after mile in terminals on this side and that side of the Atlantic Ocean and was never once hounded or harassed by anyone. I traveled light because I certainly couldn't trust any of my valuable luggages to the baggage handlers, yet my daughter traveled all the way from Togo, and her luggage was waiting for us when we arrived in Boston in perfect shape with everything in tact.

Believe it or not, my daughter and I experienced eloquent etiquette in all our travels. (It was a bit different in Paris, as I have explained earlier in this book, but the travel industry was exceptional!) This trip reminds me of these words from the pen of Paul:

Unto the pure all things are pure ... (Titus 1:15)

It makes no difference where you are; it depends on the people you meet and their intent. I know there is a "big, bad world" out there, but on this particular trip to Paris, I found I was traveling in the "grand, gracious world" I have lived in for most of my life!

## 41

## The Testimony of a Tourist

I WAS JUST 20 years old when I flew across the Pacific Ocean from America to Australia, and it wasn't until I was fifty that I flew across the Atlantic Ocean from Philadelphia to Paris. Two trips abroad in thirty years do not make me much of a tourist. Needless to say, I am no world traveler! On my first trip overseas I failed to record my observations, but as you can see, "an old dog" can learn new tricks. I have been amazed just how much I learned on my forty-hour trip to Paris and back.

On my trip to Paris, I traveled alone until I met my daughter at the Charles de Gaulle Aero port. It was a delight to be with her again. We saw as much of Paris as one can see in six hours, and we experienced, at least for a few moments, the charm and challenges of a few historic places. For the experience, I am grateful. For the shortness of the trip, I am even more thankful, for I discovered on this whirlwind tour of Paris that I am not much of a tourist!

Generally speaking, I found the airports crowded, the food tasteless, and the foreigners unhelpful. I had trouble with their signs and speech, and just ask my daughter about the water! Foreign travel is exhausting and expensive. Foreign cities are crowded and crazy. Foreign transportation is unpredictable and uncomfortable. Conclusion: foreign travel is not for me, except on those rare occasions when you need to rendezvous with your daughter in Paris! For me, a trip to Canada is all the foreign travel I really care about. Vickers's Camp on the Miramichi River is for me a better foreign adventure than Saint Michel's on the Seine River. I probably will, but I don't have to travel abroad again to be any more fulfilled than I already am.

Since I returned to the "good, old US of A," I have left the country again. As I write these afterthoughts of my trip to Paris, I am in Canada preaching to a camp of 7 to 13 year-olds: 88 of them to be exact! Getting into this country through customs was as easy as saying, "I'm an American!" I was not checked, and my personal items were not X-rayed. I didn't need a passport, and the guard at the border spoke my language. I have come to the conclusion that getting into Heaven will be more like getting into Canada than France. The trip will be shorter and the entrance easier. Saint Peter will be more concerned about me than my treasure, which I have already sent on ahead:

> But lay up for yourself treasures in heaven, where
> neither moth nor rust doth corrupt.
> (Matthew 6:20)

My conclusion as I ponder the experience of last week is that I am, nevertheless, a tourist, like it or not: "Dearly beloved, I beseech you as strangers and pilgrims . . ." (1 Peter 2:11), and I am on a time schedule: "And it is appointed unto men once to die . . ." (Hebrews 9:27). I won't be making a short visit to heaven but an eternal stay: "He that believeth on the Son hath everlasting life" (John 3:36).

## 42

## Watering Weeds

Before September 11, 2001, if someone would have asked me about air travel, I would have replied, "It is better than Aroostook County potatoes with real butter!" What made my opinion so positive was the experience I had just six weeks before the Twin Towers tragedy.

My daughter had gotten very sick on a short-term mission trip to Togo, West Africa. To make a short story shorter, I flew to Paris to rendezvous with her after her adventure in Africa. It was only my second overseas flight in fifty years. During the summer of '72, I flew to Australia to work with an Aboriginal group in the Gibson Desert. After the attacks in New York and Washington, I compared in my mind the two experiences. I discovered that it had been much harder getting in and out of America in 1972 than in 2001! America had become lax and lazy between my two transoceanic flights. What make my observations noteworthy are the similar paths this tourist took in July to what the terrorists took in September.

My travels between Europe and Ellsworth took me through Portland once and Boston twice. Despite the fact I was carrying a just-renewed passport (my old one had expired in 1977); I was never questioned on either side of the Atlantic (They didn't even stamp my passport in Paris!).

I only carried a backpack on my forty-hour odyssey, yet it was never checked once by French or American customs. Despite the fact my daughter had spent forty-four days out of the country, when we returned to Boston, her luggage was never searched. I was only a tourist, not a terrorist, but I know now how they so easily pulled this "infamy" off!

Being a minister, after 9/11 I was immediately asked, "How could God allow such a thing to happen?" Having had Paris to ponder that thought-provoking question, I now have an answer. We as a society in the last thirty years have spent too much time watering weeds! "Watering weeds?" you may ask. "What does that mean?" Little did we realize as our country grew and prospered, we were not only watering wonderful citizens that nourished and nurtured our land, but we were growing cowards (weeds) that were bent on destroying us. Recall the facts we have learned about this terrorist attack: we gave them safe haven, we taught them to fly, and we freely let them roam our "garden" at will until they found our weak points. Then they used our planes and our passengers to destroy our places and our people. When you water your garden, the only way you don't water the weeds is if you have removed the weeds before watering. America failed to root out and remove the "weeds" growing in its land before September 11th!

I for one don't blame the FBI or the CIA or any other governmental agency. I believe people were watching, but on that day in September, I recalled the profound words of an old Hebrew Psalmist:

> Except the Lord keep the city, the watchman waketh but in vain. (Psalms 127:1)

Except the gardener weeds the garden, he will end up watering weeds!

# 43

## Leaving Leaves

ONE OF THE LESSONS I learned on my adventure to Paris is the concept, condemned by Jesus, which I like to call "leaving leaves." Mark writes of the historical event this way:

> And seeing a fig tree afar off having leaves, he came, if haply he might find any thing thereon: and when he came to it, he found nothing but leaves. (Mark 11:13)

I observed on my forty-hour trip to Paris and back that this world is producing a lot of beautiful foliage, but very little beneficial fruit.

As I traveled from Ellsworth to Europe and back again, I read some of my favorite authors. Interestingly, two of them made comments on this very subject matter. Whenever God repeats something, I take notice. The first to highlight this precept to me was the great Scottish missionary, Oswald Chambers:

> Leaves of a tree are a fruit, but not the fruit; they are for the nourishment of the tree itself. That is why in the autumn, they push off and sink to the ground where they become disintegrated and are taken into the root again. The fruit proper is never for the tree itself, it is for the husbandman. Woe be to the

man who mistakes leaves for fruit! The reason Our Lord cursed the barren fig tree was because it stood as a symbol of leaves being proudly mistaken for fruit. When we mistake what we do for the fruit, we are deluded; what tells is not what we do, but what is produced by what we do!

The second to underline this concept to me was my favorite American author, Phillip Keller:

> To look at, it is a lovely tree. Ever since the first day I set eyes on this property, the handsome, young cheery tree just outside the breakfast nook aroused admiration. In spring and in summer its thick, dense foliage as a sight to behold—leaves, leaves, leaves. Season after season, we have waited patiently for its snow-white blossoms to set fruit. Few, few ever did. Last summer only a few small handfuls of stunted fruit came off this imposing tree. And this year there will be almost none to even taste. But leaves, leaves, leaves are everywhere. In quiet, pensive moments, working in the deep shade of that spreading, green-leaved tree, I have come to understand clearly what Christ meant when He uttered the simple words, "For the tree is known by his fruit!" Not by its appearance, not by its imposing size, not by its vigorous growth, and not by its abundance of leaves, leaves, leaves. Instead, the Master Gardener comes looking for fruit. The sweet fruit of His own character, His own conduct, and His own consecration made real in me!

And when I got home from Paris, the Lord led me to these words in an old church hymn written by Mrs. H. S. Lehman:

The Master is seeking a harvest, in lives He's redeemed by His blood; He seeks for the fruit of the Spirit, and works that will glorify God. Nothing but leaves for the Master, oh, how His loving heart grieves when instead of the fruit He is seeking, we offer Him nothing but leaves!

## 44

## Redeeming the Time

As I ponder again my forty-hour trip to Paris and back, I don't know if I have ever spent forty more productive hours in my life. I have come to a better understanding of what Paul meant when he wrote to the church at Ephesus these profound words:

> Redeeming the time, because the days are evil.
> (Ephesians 5:16)

Somebody has calculated that if a man lives to be sixty-five years old, he has 600,000 hours at his disposal. Forty hours seems like a drop in a bucket compared to that, yet God doesn't want us to waste any forty-hour period of our life. If you divide forty into 600,000, you have the potential of 15,000 such periods in your lifetime. Now I see the terrible waste of time I should have been redeeming. One in 15,000 doesn't seem like a lot to give to learn the lesson of the importance of always keeping eternal values in view!

Many, many years ago, I started looking at my life in terms of days, not years. I was struck by the Psalmist's challenge: "So teach us to number our days, that we may apply our hearts unto wisdom" (Psalms 90:12). On the day I left Ellsworth for Europe, it was the 18,406th day of my life; I returned on the 18,407th day of my life. When you see such huge numbers, it does cause you to ponder the great gift of time that God gives you. Fifty, my age in years, compared to 18,406 days, is a sobering reality, but as I write this remembrance, I have decided to make another mathematical calculation. My travels to the Charles de Gaulle Aero port took place between the 441,738th and 441,778th hours of my life!

I don't know if these numbers sober you up, but they have certainly affected me. By the thoughts I have written so far in this devotional, one can see the effect that this period of time has had on my life. I wonder, then, how many such periods I have wasted without listening to God. What messages have I failed to hear because I was not 'redeeming the time?' Surely we live in an evil time because our time, like no other time before us, robs us by its distractions of time spent with God. Paul told the Colossian Christian:

> Walk in wisdom toward them that are without,
> redeeming the time. (Colossians 4:5)

Once isn't what Paul was instructing! He is telling us through the inspiration of the Holy Spirit that every forty-hour period of our lives ought to be redeemed.

Richard DeHaan once wrote, "The hours, days, and years are here and gone. So whether we count them or not, let's be sure to make them count for Christ!" By now you know that I am a counter; that I love numbers. I like statistics because they are a reminder of what a man by the name of Mortenson once wrote:

> God set a goal; yet gave the choice to mortals how
> time may be spent; admonishing that worth, not
> length values time's accomplishment.

My challenge for you is to invest your time, not just spend it! And I can see clearly that I have never invested any other time better than my forty hours to Paris and back!

# 45

## Checklist for Takeoff

I AM A MAN that makes lists. The older I get the more lists I make. Perhaps it is that my mind is getting more forgetful, yet I find these lists very helpful in keeping me on schedule for my appointments. Before I headed to Paris to rendezvous with my daughter, I made this checklist to be sure I wouldn't forget anything important:

- Tickets & Travel Schedule
- Map of Paris and Ticket for Seine River Ride
- Travelers Checks & Money
- Change of Clothes & Toiletries
- Writing Paper & Pens
- Bible & Reading Books
- Jacket & Hat
- Passport & Other Documents
- Bottle of Water & Snacks
- Sunglasses & Glass Case
- Backpack to Put Everything In

As you can see, I was traveling light, but these things were all I would need to accomplish my mission to Paris.

## Checklist for Takeoff

As I ponder the list again after my return, I notice that the only item on my list that was not used was the free ticket for a ride on the Seine River in Paris. A friend in my church had taken a trip to Paris just a few weeks before I went, and he had a ticket left over. Marnie and I didn't have time to take the trip, so I returned with the ticket in my wallet. Consider with me for a moment another takeoff we as Christians are preparing for—what is on your checklist?

Peter writes:

> Seeing then that all these things shall be dissolved, what manner of persons ought ye to be in all holy conversation and godliness, looking for the hastening unto the coming of the day of God. (2 Peter 3:11–12)

When the Lord returns to retrieve His redeemed ones, what will you be carrying when you take off for heaven? We certainly know that any earthly "stuff" (Luke 17:31) will not be going! Paul tells us, "For we brought nothing into this world, and it is certain we can carry nothing out" (1 Timothy 6:7), so what ought to be on our "checklist for heaven?" Could I suggest this list compiled by Paul as given in Colossians 3:12–14?

> Put on therefore, as the elect of God, holy and beloved, bowels of mercies, kindness, humbleness of mind, meekness, longsuffering; forbearing one another, and forgiving one another, if any man have a quarrel against any: even as Christ forgave you, so also do ye. And above all these things put on charity, which is the bond of perfect ness.

Could you honestly say you are carrying this checklist in your character?

# 46

## African Jewel

WHEN I WAS A boy, I heard for the first time William Cushing's song, "Jewels":

> When He cometh, when He cometh to make up His jewels, all His jewels, precious jewels, His loved and His own; like the stars of the morning, His bright crown adorning, they shall shine in their beauty, bright gems for His crown.

It wasn't until many years later that I discovered the basis for that song was in the Bible:

> And they shall be mine, saith the Lord of hosts, in that day when I make up my jewels. (Malachi 3:17)

J. H. McConkey records this story in his devotional, *Chastening*:

> Several years ago there was found in an African mine the most magnificent diamond in the world's history. It was presented to the King of England to blaze in his crown of state. The King sent it to Amsterdam to be cut. It was put in the hands of an expert lapidary. And what do you suppose he did with it? He took this gem of priceless value and cut a notch in it. Then he struck it a hard blow with his instrument, and lo! The superb jewel lay in his hand, cleft in twain. What recklessness! What

> wastefulness! What criminal carelessness! Not so. For days and weeks that blow had been studied and planned. Drawings and models had been made of the gem; its quality, its defects, its lines of cleavage had all been studied with the minutest care. The man to whom it was committed was one of the most skilled lapidaries in the world. Do you say that blow was a mistake? Nay! It was the climax of the lapidary's skill. That blow, which seemed to ruin the superb precious stone, was in fact its perfect redemption. For from these two halves were wrought the two magnificent gems that the skilled eye of the lapidary saw hidden in the rough, uncut stone as it came from the mines. So, sometimes God lets a stinging blow fall upon your life. The nerves wince; the soul cries out in an agony of wondering protest. The blow seems to be an appalling mistake. But it is not, for you are the most priceless jewel in the world to God. And He is the most skilled lapidary in the universe. Some day you are to blaze in the diadem of the King of Kings. As you lie in His hand now, He knows just how to deal with you. Not a blow will be permitted to fall upon your shrinking soul but that the love of God permits it, and works out from it depths of blessing and spiritual enrichment unseen, and unthought-of of, by you!

My daughter, Marnie, went to Africa an uncut stone, but she returned a priceless jewel after receiving a blow from the 'lapidary of the universe.' Someone has written:

> Learn, then, sad heart, a lesson from a gem: the King of glory, passing by this way, doth seek bright jewels for His diadem. Wouldst thou for such high honour say Him nay? Lord, if Thy chastening thus can make us shine, take Thine own way, enough that it is Thine.

Let us never forget that "little children, little children, who love their Redeemer, are the jewels, precious jewels, His loved and His own!"

# 47

## Ten Days of Miracles

WHEN ONE GOES THROUGH a life-changing experience, it isn't until after that experience is over that a clear picture can be finally seen. Such was the case with my adventure to rendezvous with my daughter in Paris. Now that I have returned from that trip and had the time to replay the events back in my mind, I see better the hand of the Lord on the whole enterprise. I see now that the word from on high was, "Fear none of those things which thou shalt suffer ... and ye shall have tribulation ten days ... be thou faithful ..." (Revelation 2:10).

The Lord's events of miracles went something like this:

> Day One, July 16—Opened the heart of a postal worker to help a concerned father with the renewal of his passport so he can get out of the country to meet his daughter as she is coming home sick from West Africa.
>
> Day Two, July 17—Provided openings in the travel industry so an unexpected trip to Paris and back can be arranged through a local travel agent in Bucksport, Maine.
>
> Day Three, July 18—Kept a servant's schedule open so that a camp of kids will have a camp pastor while

the previously scheduled minister is sent off to keep a rendezvous in Paris.

Day Four, July 19—Moved the clerk at the passport office in Boston, to quickly process a passport renewal from an old 1977 expired American passport.

Day Five, July 20—Touched the hearts of family and friends with the burden of helping to finance a quick trip to Paris, France and back in 40-hours.

Day Six, July 21—Moved on the hearts of Joann, Maxine and Pricilla to encourage a reluctant father that he really needs to go to Paris and get his daughter.

Day Seven, July 22—Moved on a servant's heart to place $250 cash on the pastor's desk to reassure him that the trip to Europe would be paid and provided for.

Day Eight, July 23—Sent an email from a loving mother telling of an old friend who will send $500 for the expenses of the rescue mission.

Day Nine, July 24—Gave the concerned father an overwhelming peace about the trip—and that everything would be taken care of along his scheduled path.

Day Ten, July 25—Gets the daughter out of Africa, despite troubles with her visa, so she can rendezvoused with her Bubby at the Charles de Gaulle Aero port in Paris, France.

# 48

## A Fly on the Flight

From my seat in the back of the 737 I saw him. The pilot had just said we were cruising at 30,000 feet, and this stowaway was looking for a free lunch, besides the free ride he had already arranged. I just couldn't believe my eyes, for beside the 200-some passengers on my flight to Paris, there was also a fly!

How he had managed to get through customs I have yet to figure out. Had he simply flown in, or had he hidden among the passengers or maybe their luggage? Whatever the case, there he was in economy class waiting to attack my diner try coming down the aisle. I was impressed with his boldness and brazenness, seeing as he was flying alone—but so was I. From the language I was hearing around me, I had more in common with this fly than my fellow travelers. Most of them were heading home, or going on holiday, but my fly friend was just catching a flight to Paris, as was I. It was just a quick trip to pick up my daughter and catch the next flight home. I wondered to myself if this fly was also just along for the ride.

Perhaps he was just getting away from it all. I remember reading about a poor factory worker who used to climb a hill near his home every afternoon after a hard day's work just to get away. Perhaps this fly was just getting away from the grime and gloom and grit that were his world. Here the air was filtered and the food was gourmet. I knew he could get used to having it all to himself, or at least until somebody complained. Up to this point on our flight, I seemed to be the only one interested in the uninvited passenger.

As I struggled with the littleness one feels at 30,000 feet, my newfound friend went about his business checking all the trays for exposed sweet and sour chicken. Unconcerned that the plane could crash, or that we at best would be delayed by a storm, I thought, if he is unconcerned, why should I be concerned? So far the Good Lord had given us a smooth flight, and I had made all my arranged connections without even having to ask "a fly on the wall" where to go next! I was rebuked by his confidence and the divine travel Agent who had booked him a passage on a first-class airliner to Paris!

It is strange the things you remember after a trip. This fly on my flight to Paris was an afterthought, but it exposed how befuddled I often get with details and schedules. Instead of enjoying the ride, like my fly friend, I rushed a smooth ride and a wonderful dinner at 30,000 feet. I have become a worshiper of time experts and a lover of the schedule specialists. Paul defined them like this:

> Professing themselves to be wise, they become fools! (Romans 1:22)

Instead of finding wisdom, we have become the "wise dumb," but not my winged friend who eventually found the apple cobbler of a lady in row 32. The Wisdom of the Universe had somehow gotten me on a flight to Paris, and I was so surprised that He humbled me by showing that He could also book the same passage for a common housefly!

## 49

## Forty Hours

I HAVE MENTIONED OFTEN in this series of devotions compiled from my unexpected trip to Paris that this extraordinary event only took forty hours. (Perhaps, a good subtitle for this book.) This is the hourly timeline I kept on the trip (all events are in Maine time):

1) 7 a.m.—In Holden heading for Bangor and the bus.
2) 8 a.m.—Waiting in Concord Trailways Terminal with Coleen.
3) 9 a.m.—Passing Palmyra, writing second devotional.
4) 10 a.m.—Passing Brunswick, reading Vance Havner.
5) 11 a.m.—Passing Biddeford, working on another article.
6) 12 p.m.—Passing Topsfield, praying for next stop.
7) 1 p.m.—At US Air Terminal awaiting flight to Philly.
8) 2 p.m.—On runway at Logan Airport waiting for takeoff.
9) 3 p.m.—Landing at Philadelphia International Airport.
10) 4 p.m.—Waiting and writing at gate A7, waiting for Paris flight.
11) 5 p.m.—Standing in check-in line for Paris flight.

12) 6 p.m.—Sitting on Flight #26, which has been delayed.
13) 7 p.m.—Still sitting on Flight #26, awaiting departure.
14) 8 p.m.—On my way to Paris, watching movie "13 Days."
15) 9 p.m.—As I watch "13 Days," I have a memory forming.
16) 10 p.m.—Movie is over and I am trying to nap.
17) 11 p.m.—Talking with Canadian in the seat to my left.
18) 12 a.m.—Watching the sun rise over France.
19) 1 a.m.—Having breakfast as we descend into Paris.
20) 2 a.m.—Walking with Marnie to French customs.
21) 3 a.m.—On a RER train heading toward downtown Paris.
22) 4 a.m.—On a city bus heading toward the Eiffel Tower.
23) 5 a.m.—Buying a hat under the shadow of the Tower.
24) 6 a.m.—On Paris city bus heading back to subway.
25) 7 a.m.—On RER train heading back to de Gaulle airport.
26) 8 a.m.—In airport looking for Coleen's French tea.
27) 9 a.m.—Sitting at Gate C85 waiting flight home.
28) 10 a.m.—On plane for Boston, waiting to take off.
29) 11 a.m.—Heading home on Flight #322 talking to Marnie.
30) 12 p.m.—Marnie taking a nap on my shoulder.

31) 1 p.m.—Eating duck at 32,000 feet over the Atlantic.
32) 2 p.m.—Marnie and I talking about West Africa.
33) 3 p.m.—Watching the movie, "The Kid," very funny!
34) 4 p.m.—Just woke from a nap, missed end of movie.
35) 5 p.m.—Descending into Logan Airport in Boston.
36) 6 p.m.—Waiting at American customs for passport check.
37) 7 p.m.—Waiting at Logan to board plane for Bangor.
38) 8 p.m.—Waiting at Logan to board plane for Bangor.
39) 9 p.m.—Waiting at Logan to board plane for Bangor.
40) 10 p.m.—Over Maine writing my last thoughts of the trip.

Someone has said, "One of the best things about the future is that it only comes one hour at a time!" Paul asks this thought provoking question, "And why stand we in jeopardy every hour?" (1 Corinthians 15:30). I know now, as with my days, so are my hours in the hands of the Almighty!

## 50

## His Purpose

I ASKED IT ONCE. Then I asked it a second time. Then over and over again:

"Why am I going to Paris?"

The logical answer to this question was that I was going to rendezvous with Marnie so she wouldn't have to travel home sick from Togo, West Africa alone. But was that the real answer?

All the way to Paris and back, I asked the same question. Don't get me wrong; despite the fact Marnie didn't think I needed to come, she was glad to see me, and the special hours we spent in downtown Paris will forever be fond memories for the both of us. Yet even after we got home safely, I kept asking, "But why Lord, why?" It wasn't until I remembered this classic verse that the answer to my question became clearer:

> And we know that all things work together for good to them that love God, to them who are called according to His purpose. (Romans 8:28)

It comes down to His purpose—not mine, not my wife's, and not even my daughter's. Despite all the reassurances that Marnie could have come home alone—and we

## His Purpose

know now she could have—I was moved, motivated, and made to go to Paris. Parents and parishioners had encouraged me, but I still wanted to know why God wanted me to go? I wanted to know His purpose! After much meditation and consideration, these are the thoughts I eventually arrived at concerning "why?"

1) I considered the process of His purpose—For ten days, every event, action, and conversation pointed to the fact that this trip, for whatever purpose, was foreknown and preordained as part of my future. Despite its rarity in my life, it was as if I was going to Perham (my hometown), not Paris! "The steps of a good man are ordered by the Lord: and he delighteth in his way" (Psalms 37:23).

2) I considered the people of His purpose—The key people were in my family, for example—a promise early in the summer to my wife that if Marnie got into any trouble on her trip, I would be prepared to go after her, anywhere. The advice of trusted friends and brethren also proved very important. "Where no counsel is, the people fall: but in the multitude of counselors there is safety" (Proverbs 11:14).

3) I considered the providence of His purpose—How God worked out the passport renewal; arranged the tickets to fit perfectly with my daughter's schedule despite being arranged months apart; how he brought in money for the trip from unexpected places and people. "Faithful is he that calleth you, who also will do it" (1 Thessalonians 5:24).

4) I considered the protection of His purpose—It is dangerous to fly, and Paris is a dangerous place, yet "if God be for us, who can be against us?" (Romans 8:31).
5) I considered the promise of His purpose—"All things work together for good!" All I know is that I am back from this trip, and as I write, all things did work together for good!

Sometimes in life you just have to put your faith in God's hand and go, even when you have nothing to go on!

# Postlude

IN THE LATTER YEARS of my life, I have been a stickler for getting there on time, staying on time, and knowing what time it is. I have also pretty much kept to my own schedule, but in the last two days I have been at the mercy of airlines and bus lines and train lines. I have traveled through six time zones both ways, but I have kept my wristwatch on 'Maine time' and my pocket watch on "Paris time." As I write this, I am flying over Maine in an American Eagle aircraft heading for home after a marathon that has taken me to Bangor, Portland, Boston, Philadelphia, Paris, and Boston again, and soon back to Bangor, all in just forty hours. I have been impressed just how closely my schedule has matched their schedule, or should I say HIS schedule?

I, like others, have an inherent weakness and that being the anticipation of delays and cancellations that rarely happens. As I look back over the hours, I didn't miss an important connection, but in my imagination before this trip, I failed to arrive many times. As usual, I conjured up hang-ups and hold-ups! There is no end to what my mind can dream up; I even had the plane crashing a time or two!

I often have been like the women friends of Jesus heading for His tomb, wondering who would roll the stone away (Mark 16:3); it had already been taken care of! All my fears and apprehensions about this trip were taken care of long before I got to any major crossroad. And as the Lord was clearing my way, He was also clearing the way for my daughter. When she got to customs in Togo, she discovered that she had been in the country illegally for fourteen days. Somebody had made a mistake, and because it was in French, nobody noticed it. But there was nothing to fear or fret or fuss about because God had his angel—a heavenly helper—in the Lome Airport to get her through the bottleneck.

If I have learned anything on my trip to Paris it is to trust in the Lord's angels to clear the way ahead. God's representatives keep us on schedule even if they have to move heaven and earth to get us where we ought to be. Paul warns us, "Be not forgetful to entertain strangers: for thereby some have entertained angels unawares" (Hebrews 13:2). Whether that customs agent in Lome or my traveling companion from Canada ... well out of my element and way beyond my comfort zone, I discovered that God has plenty of helpers scattered around the world, and they appear to us as simple people who drive buses and fly planes and stamp passports!

I hope you have enjoyed my memoirs from my *Rendezvous in Paris*, and that the next time you travel; you will be on the lookout for the Lord's helpers. (By the way, my daughter is fine with no ill effects from her Togo diseases. I have come to believe the real reason I went to Paris was to write a book! I will let you be the judge of that!)

Barry Blackstone
July 26, 2001

www.ingramcontent.com/pod-product-compliance
Lightning Source LLC
Chambersburg PA
CBHW070500090426
42735CB00012B/2638